New Testament Psalms

New Testament Psalms

Praises for the Church of the Lord Jesus Christ

Rev. Joseph D. Carota

TATE PUBLISHING
AND ENTERPRISES, LLC

Published by Tate Publishing & Enterprises, LLC
127 E. Trade Center Terrace | Mustang, Oklahoma 73064 USA
1.888.361.9473 | www.tatepublishing.com

Tate Publishing is committed to excellence in the publishing industry. The company reflects the philosophy established by the founders, based on Psalm 68:11,
"The Lord gave the word and great was the company of those who published it."

Cover design by Arjay Grecia
Interior design by Jomel Pepito

Published in the United States of America

ISBN: 978-1-62902-912-2
Religion / Christian Life / Devotional
15.03.16

Dedication

There have been many people who have passed through my life who have had an effect on me and who have contributed to my being who I am today in Christ Jesus.

Many passed through without knowing they had any effect on my life at all. Others might have guessed that something was being done in me. But for all of those that have contributed to my life, I thank you.

Those who have gone on to be with the Lord:

My parents: Anthony Sr. and Concetta Carota who adopted me, brought me up in the nurture and admonition of the Lord, and who showed Jesus to me in innumerable ways. My knowledge of the Bible and my love of the Psalms, in particular, were instilled in me by my mother.

Pastor Melvin Dorr, who was my pastor while I was growing up and who put up with a lot from a rambunctious me over the years.

Mr. and Mrs. Truax who were the leaders of our youth group and our Bible quiz team coaches.

Mrs. Oscar Osterberg, my first vocal coach and music teacher. She taught me not only how to sing but how to communicate through music.

Pastor Fisher, who taught me how to minister to people, how to behave in the pulpit, and how to deal with people at the altar.

Dr. Johns, dean of Central Bible College, who showed me that someone can be a man of God and an intellectual at the same time without either side of the man suffering.

Those who are still living and awaiting heaven:

Dan Abbatello, Rob Fisher, and Nathan DeGeasare who ministered with me as The King's Messengers, a vocal Gospel group, way back when I was sixteen to seventeen years old.

Joe Lima, leader of the youth group after I received the Holy Ghost.

Rev. Dennis DeLine, one of my roommates in Bible college, my confidant, and best friend from that time to the present and someone I can always count on for godly counsel.

Rev. Edward and Diana Gentz, who loved me in a time of my life when I was very unlovable.

Rev. Anthony Langston, senior pastor who taught me a lot when I was his associate pastor.

Rev. Richard Reese, who utilized my ministry during a very transitional part of my life.

Rev. Mark Fowler, who has encouraged me in innumerable ways and has had an incredible impact on my life and ministry. For his friendship, his pastoral care and his spiritual influence on my life and ministry I could never thank him enough.

Only eternity will show all of what has been accomplished because of the influence of these people named above and those many, many others I have not named.

Special thanks to Minister Michele Bernier of the National Association of Christian Ministers, who encouraged me to seek the publication of this work after she read some of these "Psalms."

Special thanks to Mack "Bear" Murray, a friend who has stood by me and has helped in innumerable ways.

Finally, a grateful thanks to Tate Publishing for their willingness to put this work into print and for seeing its potential to affect other people's lives and hopefully bringing them closer to the Lord Jesus Christ.

May God give a special blessing to all who have affected my ministry and my life.

New Testament Psalms: Praises for the Church of the Lord Jesus Christ

The writings in this book are not truly "psalms." The Psalms of the Bible were written as songs used in worship. The psalms of this collection are not songs but praises, prayers, and some are just calling out to God, but they are still used in worship!

The main difference of these psalms from those in the Bible is that these center around the Lord Jesus Christ and His work of atonement; His life, death, and resurrection; as well as the working of the Holy Spirit within the individual and within the Body of Christ, which of course all took place long after the Old Testament Psalms were written.

I grew up my whole life reading, studying, and memorizing scripture from the King James Version of the Bible. When I started comparing and using other biblical translations I noticed many differences but nothing stood out to me so strongly as the difference in the *sounding* of the Psalms. They just didn't sound as…majestic or as grandiose or regal to my ear outside of the King James English. To many, I am sure, that will seem foolish. Many see no major difference. But I do. And because I do, when I started to write my own psalms, they just came out in King James English, and I kept that format.

These psalms have been written in the Davidic style in King James English but with an understanding of the Lord Jesus Christ as the physical embodiment of God, God in the flesh, the incarnate One, who has provided salvation for mankind through His sacrificial death and His glorious resurrection from the dead to ascend as the perfect atonement for the sins of mankind and thus the focus of the praises within these psalms. These psalms include some actual scripture, some hymn stanzas, and other quotes drawn from my memory and my heart but are mostly just personal praise and soul-felt worship.

It is my prayer that you will be blessed when reading this work, and I pray that you may find these pieces of personal worship useful in your own personal worship of the One who is and was and is to come.

Maranatha!

—Rev. Joseph D. (JD) Carota

Foreword

If you've had the opportunity of reading *Psalms Now* by *Leslie* F. *Brandt*; then you will enjoy *New Testament Psalms: Praises for the Church of the Lord Jesus Christ.* God's Word tells us in John 1:14;

> "And the Word became flesh, and dwelt among us, and we saw His glory, glory as of the only begotten from the Father, full of grace and truth." (nasv)

That's exactly what Rev. Joseph D. (JD.) Carota has done. You will find throughout these writings the overwhelming presence of the Lord Jesus Christ. In reading the *New Testament Psalms,* you will experience:

- An inner Joy
- A spiritual fulfillment of Peace
- A dancing heart with shouts of Praise
- And a voice that audibly and silently utters prayers of gratefulness

The message in these pages will enlighten the Christian to heights of worship. You will find your soul being uplifted and your heart encouraged. I believe this to be an essential read for the Believer in these last days. With evil all around and the pressures of this ungodly society crowding in on the sons and daughters of God, Jesus must be our focus. The *New Testament Psalms* is a tool that will help us achieve victory in our lives. We must remember that God inhabits the praises of His people. And we must praise Him.

Why do I believe so strongly about this book? Hebrews 10:19-24 tells us:

"Therefore, brethren, since we have confidence to enter the holy place by the blood of Jesus, by a new and living way which He inaugurated for us through the veil, that is, His flesh, and since *we have* a great priest over the house of God, let us draw near with a sincere heart in full assurance of faith, having our hearts sprinkled clean from an evil conscience and our bodies washed with pure water. Let us hold fast the confession of our hope without wavering, for He who promised is faithful; and let us consider how to stimulate one another to love and good deeds, not forsaking our own assembling together, as is the habit of some, but encouraging one another; and all the more as you see the day drawing near." (Nasv)

We are to stimulate one another as brothers and sisters in the Lord; building up each other for the strengthening of the body of Christ. In acknowledging the Lord Jesus Christ in these "Psalms"; is to rightfully say; "And the Word became flesh and dwelt among us..." I encourage you on this note: read the words of this book and allow God's Spirit to edify your total being through Worship, Praise, and Prayer.

—Reverend Mark Fowler
Pastor, Johnstown Church of the Nazarene

Psalm 1

Give ear to my call, O Lord Most High; hear me when I call upon thy name; For thou art my God; thou art the center of my life.

I was lost, yea, I was dead in my trespasses and sins until I heard the glorious Gospel of the Lord Jesus Christ, and in hearing, my soul came alive within me. I called upon the name of Jesus and He hath redeemed me. The blood of Calvary washed over me, cleansing me, washing me, changing me and taking all my sins from me never to be remembered against me again.

How can I give thee praise enough for my salvation through thy blood, O Lord my God? How can this poor tongue of mine give thee the glory thou art worthy of?

The Lord, He is God. There is none like him. His name is majestic: His name is above every name. O great God, my Savior, my Lord, my Redeemer, my Jesus, I worship thee for thou alone art worthy of my praise, for thou alone hast freed me from sin.

I was lost. I was undone. I was sinking into the mire of despair.

I called upon the name of Jesus, and He saved my soul and brought me into a new land of glory and joy.

Hear ye nations and give ear ye peoples of the earth for the blood of Jesus still saves from sin. Call upon the name of the Lord. For if thou shalt confess with thy mouth the Lord Jesus Christ, and believe in thy heart that God hath raised him from the dead, thou shalt be saved.

Psalm 2

I have a song. My soul sings. Thou, O Lord, art the melody within me.

Give forth thy song, O my soul; sing, rejoice, be glad, shout, dance, be happy, O song within me for He who is thy salvation and hath given to thee the song welling up within thee is thy God.

I have a song. My soul sings. Thou, Lord Jesus art the harmony within me.

My song is the song of the redeemed. My melody is the joy of the blood-bought.

O, soul, rejoice in Majesty. O, soul, sing and resound the glory of the Crucified One; for He hath bought thee with His own blood. He hath given His body to be broken; His wounds heal thee. Therefore, O my soul, sing unto the Lord the blood-bought anthem. Sing Hallelujah to the Risen Redeemer.

The saints of the Lord sing glory to His name. The people of the Name lift up their voices to the Exalted One; He who sits upon the heavens and rides upon the winds.

I have a song. My soul sings.

Sing O my soul. Sing and be glad; for thou hast been made a joint heir with Christ Jesus and with him thou shalt reign forever within His glory, clothed in His righteousness. Sing to the Lord the new song of the blood-bought. Salvation is come and thou art sanctified.

Psalm 3

The Lord reigns; let His name be praised.
The Lord reigns; shout unto thy God O ye people of the Lord.
The Lord reigns; let the heavens tremble.
The Lord reigns; let the mountains clap their hands and rejoice.
The Lord reigns; let His glory resound.
The Lord reigns; let His name be exalted.
Holy, holy, holy, hear the chorus of the seraphim. Glory and honor, dominion and power, exaltation, majesty, and praise to the One who is and was and is to come.
The Lord reigns; give Him glory O earth.
The Lord reigns; let all creation well up with singing.
The Lord reigns; He is God alone.
The Lord reigns; Jesus is His name.
The Lord reigns; saints of the Lord give Him honor.
The Lord reigns; His majesty shines throughout the whole earth.
The heavens declare the glory of God and the firmament showeth His handiwork.

Trees and flowers; mountains and streams; hillsides of grass and budding magnolias; oceans and all within them; rivers and deltas; beasts of the forest and all animals and fowl; praise thy Creator; give praise to the One who spoke thee into existence.

There is none like thee O Lord, there is none like thee.

The Lord reigns; let my voice be lifted and let His name be praised.

Psalm 4

Great is the Lord and righteous is His name. He is exalted in majesty and His kingdom will never end.

Thou, O Lord, art a God above gods. There is none like thee. Thou hast a name above all names, for thou, O Lord Christ hast conquered death and hell. Thou hast overcome the enemy by thine own sacrifice.

Thou hast offered thy body as the sacrifice Lamb and though thou didst die thou art alive again forevermore.

Thy praise shall ring from thy people, O Lord. The name of Jesus shall be exalted.

Before thee we bow great Master of the Universe. It is to thee that we give praise.

Shout to the Lord O ye people of the Lord. Give praise to His name for He is great. Shout to the Lord and give praise to the Lord Jesus, you blood-bought throngs. Give praise to him. Give praise.

Sing, dance, shout, and exult in His righteousness you Spirit-filled host. He has sanctified thee with His Spirit and by His Most Holy Spirit hath he given thee life, yea, He hath raised thee into the heavenlies as sons of God: Bought with a price, raised to new life, and adopted into the family of God as joint heirs with Christ Jesus.

Give praise to the Lord. Give Jesus all glory, honor, and adoration.

Psalm 5

O, my soul, be not cast down. Though thy bones may ache and thy muscles seemeth useless; though thou canst not do as thou might wish, do not be ensnared in self-regret.

Though thy head may be grayed and thou art slowed, thou art not yet in the grave, so lift up thy heart and see the glory that surrounds thee even in thine infirmity.

Though thou mayest feel that thou canst not be as in thy youth, thou are yet vital in the Lord thy God.

Jesus holds thy hand; yea, He doth unhold thee in all thy doings. Thou art not alone. Thou canst not be alone, for the Lord thy God, even HaShem, is nigh thee continually.

Hath He not promised thee that He would never leave thee nor forsake thee? Hath He not promised that in His presence is fullness of joy? Doth not His word say unto thee that weeping may endure for a night but that joy cometh in the morning? Hath He not said that He is to thee YHWH-Rapha, YHWH-Jirah, thy healer, thy provider?

Canst thou want for more than He is to thee? Canst thou say to the Lord, thou art not enough? Thou knowest right well that the Lord is all sufficient unto thee. Thou knowest that He hath said that thou art engraved on the palm of His hand.

The nail prints testify to thee, along with thy name engraved on His palm, that thou belongest to the Lord and that Jesus is thine own in all assurance.

Do not be cast down, O my soul. Thou belongest to God. Thou art in the arms of Jesus thy Lord and thy God.

Thou art the sheep of His pasture and in His arms doth He uphold thee day and night.

Therefore be lifted up. Thou art the Lord's. Be upheld even as He upholdeth thee. Rejoice, for thou knowest that neither height nor depth, nor any other creature, shall be able to separate thee from the love of God that is in Christ Jesus thy Lord.

Psalm 6

Mine eyes behold a hill, silhouetted against a darkened sky. Mine eyes behold a cross standing upon the mount of Calvary.

Upon this hill, this mount, this place of suffering, mine ears can still hear a gasping, dying voice cry, "It is finished."

Finished for me; Finished for all time; Finished so that all who call upon the name of the Lord may be saved; Finished to claim the victory over death, hell, and the grave; Finished so that He might have a name that is above every name.

In mine heart, His voice rings, "This was for thee." In my spirit I hear, "I love thee with an overwhelming love."

The work is finished: His love remains. His Spirit is strong and His glory shines forth in all the blood-bought Hosts of Saints.

Give praise to the Lord Jesus for His love spent sacrifice. Give glory to He who was and is and is to come, the Lord Christ.

He hath finished the work. He hath sealed me with His Holy Spirit of promise and unto Him my soul resounds with His praises.

Psalm 7

I wake to a chorus of singing; the birds of the heavens give glory to their Creator. Mine eyes open and the light of thy majesty shines from the sun.

When I wake; thou art with me. When I lay me down to rest; behold, thou art with me. Thou dost hold me in thine arms, day and night; throughout my life thou holdest me.

Thou art my sustenance, O Lord my Father. Thou art the full joy of my life and the lifter of my head.

O, Lord Christ, how I rejoice in thee; thou majestic Ruler of all; thou glorious resurrected One; thou who hast washed me in thine own blood that I might be acceptable in the beloved.

Morning brings glory to thee, O Lord. Evening sees thee enthroned in majesty. Night shines brilliant as noon day because the Lord is Lord of all and there is none beside Him.

How glorious thou art, O King of the Universe; how great is thy name.

I will give voice to the majesty of the Lord Christ for His awesomeness is beyond the understanding of man; yet thou hast chosen to tabernacle as one of us; thou didst take on flesh and thou didst live as one of thine own creation, sacrificing thyself for the sins of thy handiwork. Yet thou didst rise from the dead and Thou dost live forevermore.

Shout to the Lord O ye people of the Lord for He hath redeemed thee from destruction. His blood hath bought thee a place at His table.

When I do lay me down to rest, I breathe thy name and thou comest and doth take thy place by my side holding me through the night.

When I wake in the morning, thou art there, and I lift mine eyes to thee and give thee the praise of my heart for I love thee Lord and I give all my days to thee.

Psalm 8

He rides upon the winds. His voice breaks the waves upon the rocks. His footsteps shatter the mountains.

He is a great and awesome God; there is none like Him.

There are those that are called gods; they are but stone or wood, and the imagination of men's minds. There is no substance to them. They have no power. They cannot see. They cannot speak. They are silent and dumb.

But the Lord, He is God. He hath spoken the worlds into existence. It was by His word that all exists.

But man He hath formed with His own hands. It is the Lord who hath made man in His own image. In the image of the Lord hath man been made.

His hands formed from the dust of the earth His first Adam and He breathed into man the breath of lives and man became a living soul.

Clap your hands all ye nations, shout unto God with the voice of triumph; For the Lord is great and greatly to be praised.

Lift up thy voice, O ye daughters of Zion; arise, shine for thy light hath come. Wave the banners and shout for joy, for thy God hath provided thee with salvation. The Lord hath made thee accepted in the beloved.

The mountains tremble; the seas roar. The earth shakes at the presence of the Most High.

Thy Messiah hath come. The Lord hath said that He would be a light unto the Gentiles and a hope to the nations.

Thus is the Lord Christ. Jesus hath brought the salvation of the Lord to those who were afar off. To those who were not part of the nation of Israel; to those outside the household of faith, hath he grafted in by His own blood. He hath adopted those who have come to Him by faith.

For the Lord loved the world so much that He hath given His only begotten Son that whosoever believeth in Him shall not perish but have everlasting life.

Give praise to the Lord, O ye people. Shout unto God for the glory of His salvation in the Lord Jesus Christ.

Psalm 9

Blessed is the man who walketh not in the ways of sinners nor sitteth in the seat of the scornful.

Blessed is the man who holds his heart open to God, who sees all of man's ways.

Blessed is the sanctified man, who hath been filled with the Spirit of the Lord.

Blessed is the man who acknowledges the supremacy of God; who calls upon the Lord in all things.

Blessed are the pure in spirit for they shall see God.

Blessed art thou when men shall persecute thee and say all manner of evil against thee falsely for the name of the Lord's sake.

Blessed are the blood-bought for they shall inherit the presence of Jesus.

Blessed are the poor in spirit for theirs is the kingdom of heaven.

Blessed is the man who delights in the Word of the Lord; who spends his days meditating on the knowledge of God.

Blessed is he who wakes to greet the Presence in the morning and who sleepeth at night surrounded by the glory of the Lord.

Blessed are they who mourn for they shall be comforted.

Blessed is the man who seeks the Spirit in all his ways; who gives to God all that he is.

Blessed are they who give praise to the Lord for His goodness, His faithfulness, and His Love.

Blessed are all they who see the love of the Lord shining in the person of the Lord Jesus and who acknowledge His Kingship and His majesty.

Blessed is the man whose heart belongs to Jesus for he shall, in his flesh, see God.

Psalm 10

Hear me when I call, O God of my righteousness: thou hast enlarged me when I was in distress; have mercy upon me, and hear my prayer.

Give ear to my words, O Lord, consider my meditations.

I shall turn to the Lord in all my ways and give voice to my longings for my God.

Lead me, O Lord, in thy righteousness; show unto thy servant the ways of thy Spirit.

Jesus shall reign over all the earth; His majesty shall shine as the sun and His glory as the brilliance of midday.

Come, Holy Ghost, our hearts inspire, let us thine influence prove; source of the old prophetic fire, be thou a fountain of life and love.

O God, through the Spirit we shall know, if thou within us shine, and sound, with all thy saints below, the depths of love divine.

Hear me, O God, and let my words come before thee in the love that is within me for thee.

I am in need of thy Presence, O thou Most High. Bring to me thy nearness and let me know thee more. Let me know thee in the power of thy resurrection.

Love divine, all loves excelling, joy of heaven, to earth come down; fix in us thy humble dwelling; all thy faithful mercies crown! Jesus thou art all compassion, pure, unbounded love thou art; visit us with thy salvation; enter every trembling heart.

O, Jesus, my God, my Lord, my Redeemer, my all in all, I give thee praise for thy unbounded love for me; for thy sacrifice upon Calvary and for thy rising from the dead. For thou art my God and all the days of my life I will give thee praise.

Psalm 11

Behold, what manner of love the Father hath bestowed upon us, that we may be called the children of God.

For we are His workmanship; The creation of His hands.

He hath made us accepted in the beloved by His own blood.

Thy love, O God, hath drawn me to thee. Thy love hath given me life.

For the love of God is shed abroad in our hearts by the Holy Ghost; and thy love brings me to thee.

We are His people; His children; His habitation.

The Lord hath brought us nigh to Himself by the blood of a new and everlasting covenant; the covenant of His blood.

Calvary is ultimate love displayed.

See there, ye people of the earth; see and behold how thy God hath provided for thee escape from sin and death.

Behold and let faith arise in thine heart; the price hath been paid. Sin's penalty is satisfied.

O, Lord my God, how can I give thee the praises that thou art worthy of?

May the Lord direct thy hearts into the love of God and into the patient waiting for Christ. For His return is nigh. Look up, ye people of the Lord and look for His glorious return. He hath loved thee with an everlasting love and His love will bring Him back for His church; for those washed in His blood and anointed and sealed with His Holy Spirit. He that saith, I know him, and keepeth not his commandments, is a liar, and the truth is not in him. But whoso keepeth His word, in him verily is the love of God perfected:

Ye servants of God, your Master proclaim, and publish abroad His wonderful name; the name all-victorious of Jesus extol, His kingdom is glorious and rules over all.

Blessed art thou, O Lord, our God, King of the Universe; and blessed is thy Most Holy Name forever.

Then let us adore and give Him His right, all glory and power, all wisdom and might; All honor and blessing with angels above, and thanks never ceasing and infinite love.

Psalm 12

Give ear to my words, O Lord, consider my meditation.

Hearken unto the voice of my cry, my King, and my God: for unto thee will I pray. My voice shalt thou hear in the morning, O Lord; in the morning will I direct my prayer unto thee, and will look up.

For thou art not a God that hath pleasure in wickedness: neither shall evil dwell with thee.

Thou dost not regard iniquity as faultless; thou art a God, a righteous Judge and thou doth see truly the blackness of the heart of man. Thou art aware of the depths of depravity within thy creation, the offspring of Adam.

But let all those that put their trust in thee rejoice: let them ever shout for joy, because thou defendest them: let them also that love thy name be joyful in thee. For thou, Lord, wilt bless the righteous; with favour wilt thou compass him as with a shield.

The Lord shall judge the people: judge me, O Lord, according to my righteousness, and according to mine integrity that is in me.

Oh let the wickedness of the wicked come to an end; but establish the just: for the righteous God trieth the hearts and reins.

My defence is of God, which saveth the upright in heart.

God judgeth the righteous, and God is angry with the wicked every day.

Thou art holy, O Lord; thy name, thy being, all that thou art is holy.

Let the people of God arise and proclaim the holiness of the Lord, the Christ; for in Him is all the fullness of the Godhead bodily; and in Him is all righteousness displayed.

He is a great and awesome God. There is none beside Him; there is none like thy God, O Zion.

Arise, ye children of the Blood; arise and present thy bodies a living sacrifice, which is they reasonable service.

The Lord is holy; be thou therefore holy, ye people of the Lord for He, thy God is holy.

Display His righteousness within thee, O people of the Lord; show forth His holiness wrought in thee by His Most Holy Spirit.

O Lord, our Lord, how excellent is thy name in all the earth! Who hast set thy glory above the heavens.

Out of the mouth of babes and sucklings hast thou ordained strength because of thine enemies, that thou mightest still the enemy and the avenger.

But thou art holy, O thou that inhabitest the praises of Israel.

Our fathers trusted in thee: they trusted, and thou didst deliver them. They cried unto thee, and were delivered: they trusted in thee, and were not confounded.

The Lord loveth His people; He hath regard for the righteous, but the arrogant doth He despise.

Present unto the Lord holiness and honor; give to the Lord the majesty due to His glorious, almighty name.

The Lord, is the Lord of Host; Christ Jesus is His name; and His glory shines throughout eternity and shall be displayed in all the earth when He is crowned King of all.

Psalm 13

How long wilt thou tarry, O Lord? How long wilt thou delay thy returning?

How long will thy people wait for the trumpet to sound? How long wilt thou hold back the Archangel from blowing the shofar?

Thy Word doth say, "For the Lord himself will descend from heaven with a shout. With the voice of the archangel and with the trump of God; and the dead in Christ shall rise first, and those that are alive and remain shall be caught up together with them in the clouds to meet the Lord in the air. And so shall we ever be with the Lord."

How long, O Lord?

We wait for thee, O God. Thy people long for thee.

Those of white robes; those blood-washed hosts; those clothed in thine own righteousness and displaying thy holiness to the nations wait for thee.

Yet, even as we desire to be with thee, O Master of Life; even as we long to be with thee for eternity, our hearts cry, "Not yet, Lord." For we have loved ones who need thee. There are still too many who have not heard thy word. There are still too many who are not ready for thy return; who have not surrendered their hearts, who have not been blood-washed.

Save, O God. Save those of our hearts that need thee.

We long to be with thee, O Christ. We long to worship thee throughout the endless ages of eternity and yet we desire our loved ones with us. We desire the unsaved to come to know thee.

How long wilt thou tarry, O Lord? How long wilt thou delay thy return? Yet a little while, Lord; yet one more soul, Savior. Yet one more added to the Kingdom ere the trumpet sound, and the heavens break open and thou comest back for thy Church. Yet one more, Lord.

But in all, my heart cries out to my Lord, my Redeemer, my Jesus, maranatha Lord. Maranatha! Even so, come Lord Jesus.

Psalm 14

Be not cast down O my soul. The Lord reigns.

Look to the heavens and behold His glory.

The enemies of my soul circle around me continually and compass me about; they seek to destroy me, yea, they seek me as a roaring lion seeketh whom he may devour.

The heathen rage and the ungodly rise up; but the power of the Holy Ghost shines forth in righteousness in those that call upon the name of Jesus; to those who call upon the name of the Lord in faith believing.

Let the Church arise; Let those of the Blood stand strong in the power of God.

O ye people of the Lord present thy bodies as a living sacrifice, acceptable unto God, which is thy reasonable service.

The Lord speaks and the mountains tremble. The voice of the Most High goes forth and creation quakes. The oceans rise and the waves role. The thunder rumbles in the distance and lightning streaks across the heavens, at the command of the Lord. The winds blow and the tempest quickens for the word of the Lord hath spoken it.

But the people of the Lord have a strong tower in God. The Israel of God have a full refuge in His arms; yea, in His bosom do they rest and become secure for the Lord is their God and His ways are surety and righteousness.

Psalm 15

Shout to the north; lift your voice and cry to the south; call forth to the east and west that Jesus Christ is Lord above all and that His kingdom shall never end.

Raise your voices ye people of the Blood and sound out the glory of the Lord your God.

Lift your hands ye people; lift your hands and praise the Lord.

Give praise to God for He is worthy of all thine adoration and all thy praise.

Hallelujah! To the Lamb. Hallelujah! To the Risen One. Hallelujah! To the One who is and was and is to come.

Glory and honor, dominion and power, adoration, majesty and praise to the Lord Christ; Glory to His name. Praise to His glorious name.

Let all the people of the Lord lift up their voices and shout the glory of the Lord to all the nations. Let the name of the Lord be praised.

Stand up and shout ye people. Shout unto God with the voice of triumph; For the Lord hath done marvelous things. He hath bought for thee thy salvation, yea, His own Blood hath purchased thee from destruction.

He hath triumphed over death and hell. He is victorious over sin and death.

Oh give praise to the Lord for His abundant grace. His mercy shall cover thee all the days of thy life for thou art engraved on the palm of His hand as His child.

Thy grace, O God is wondrous to thy people. Amazing is the grace of our God.

Psalm 16

Praise ye the Lord. Praise Him in the heavens. Praise Him, O ye people of the earth.

Give glory to the One who sitteth upon the Throne and unto the Lamb, who is worthy of all praise.

The Lord rules in judgment. His justice covers the mountains, His righteousness covers the seas. The heathen hear thereof and tremble, for the Lord is sovereign over all; His greatness is over all the earth.

Glory and honor be unto the name of our God for the Lord Jesus Christ is His name and all glory is His.

Shout and dance before the Lord. Worship and adore Him all ye people.

Let the blood-bought give praise to the Risen One; to the one who was dead and lives now and forever and ever.

Hallelujah to the Lamb of God; to the Lamb who was slain and now lives.

Hallelujah to the Almighty God; Sovereign of the universe.

Praise ye the Lord. Praise Him all ye people. Praise him mountains and forests, seas and rivers, valleys and hills, give glory to the Lord.

Jesus shall reign over all the earth. His glory shall be revealed to all people for we shall behold Him as He is, and in His glory shall He be shown to all the inhabitants of the earth.

Psalm 17

Thy name, O Lord, is like water in the desert; as bright sunshine in winter; like the new growth of budding trees and flowers in springtime.

When my heart is heavy, or the turmoil of life weighs me down and my spirit is dismal, I breathe thy name and I am refreshed.

When pain consumes me, and my old bones ache, thy name, O Jesus, brings joy to my heart and healing to my body.

Thy name, O God, is a strong and mighty tower; the righteous run into it and are saved.

Thy name doth save me; thy name doth uphold me; thy name is solace in a storm and a refuge for my flagging spirit.

Blessed is the name of the Lord; the Lord God of Israel; the Sovereign of all creation; the majestic King of Glory.

Blessed is the Lord Jesus Christ; the Risen One; the Conqueror of death hell and the grave.

Blessed is thy name, O God, for thy glory doth cover the earth; thy majesty is seen in all the works of thy hand. The mountains tremble before the name of the Lord. The trees clap their hands in praise to thy glory and to the majesty of thy name.

O, for a thousand tongues to give glory to the Lord; O that I could give to the Lord the praises due to His majesty and His name.

He is glorious; he is awesome in power; His name is above all names.

Let the name of Jesus be praised; let the name of the Lord be exalted forever. Let the people praise His glorious dominion and the power of the name of Jesus.

Psalm 18

I cried unto the Lord, and He heard my voice.

How great is the mercy of the Lord?

In my prison I lifted my cry to the Lord, and He released me.

How great is the grace of the Lord?

My soul failed within me; I became as a dead man, yet the Lord was with me.

How great is the Presence of the Lord.

My sins laid me waste. Mine iniquity separated me from the Lord my God.

How great is the compassion of the Lord?

The Lord became flesh and dwelt among us. He, who reigns in glory, became as one of His own creation and was born as the Son of Man.

How great is the providence of the Lord?

In His flesh he provided my redemption. By His blood He provided my salvation.

How great is the love of the Lord?

The Lord lives. Let the people rejoice.

Jesus is alive. Let all the earth give praise.

I lifted my voice to the glorious One, and He saved my soul.

How great is the mercy of the Lord?

In my despair I called, "O, Lord, I am in need," and He came to me.

How great is the grace of the Lord?

I was alone, bound, and sick in heart and soul. But the Lord covered me with His blood and my soul was lifted up.

How great is the Presence of the Lord?

Mine enemies surrounded me. I was in danger and great peril, but the Lord defended me and His strong right arm upheld me.

How great is the compassion of the Lord?

My life was lacking. I came short of the glory of God, but God, in His Spirit came upon me and sanctified me. In His entirety, He sanctified me.

How great is the love of the Lord?

Psalm 19

The Blood hath won at Calvary. The Blood hath finished the work. The Blood hath brought back the possibility of Eden.

O, Lord, thy Blood hath made all things new. Thou hast been prepared as a sacrifice and thy Blood hath won all victory.

I live because thou didst die. I live because thou has risen and art alive forevermore.

What can wash away my sin? Nothing but the Blood of Jesus? What can make me whole again? Nothing, but the Blood of Jesus?

I praise thee O God for thy love. Thy love hast been displayed in thine own wounds. Thy hands and feet, thy torn and mangled body, thy riven side hath made devils flee; it hath made up a Church, a Body of thine own people which shall forever be victorious because of thy Blood.

Anoint me, O God, to break out against the gates of hell. Anoint me, O Lord Jesus, to stand up and raise the standard of the Blood-stained banner. Anoint me, O God, to rage against the onslaught of the enemy and break out in righteousness and holiness and take back what is rightfully thine and thy Kingdoms'. No longer will the Church lay placidly by and allow the enemy to conquer thy territory. No longer will thy people sit by and not take up thy charge to go to the nations and make disciples, baptizing them and seeing them growing into thine own image, O great Lord my God and my Savior.

Thy people shall rise up. Thy people shall shout thy praise. Thy people shall take thy power and thine anointing and go into the world and show thy might and glory. We shall break down the strongholds of the enemy and take thy Blood against the oppressed in Jesus' name. Thy people shall display thy power by thy Spirit's infilling. Thy people shall proclaim thy Kingdom come to the nations and devils shall flee before the onslaught of thy power and glory displayed through thy people anointed by thy power and tabernacled by thy Spirit.

Holy is the Lord and holy shall be thy people, in thy name and by thy power. Thy Spirit shall flood over the nations and righteousness in Jesus' name shall be shown until thou comest again. Glory be to the conquering King of Glory.

Who is this King of glory? The Lord Jesus, strong and mighty; the Lord Jesus, mighty in battle. He is the King of Glory; and He hath won the victory by His own Blood.

Psalm 20

All glory, laud, and honor be unto Christ the King, who lives and reigns on high and is exalted above all gods.

For the gods of the earth are the imagination of men's minds; the work of their hands. They are idols of gold and silver, bronze, stone, and wood. They see not neither do they have understanding.

But the Lord, He is God. He alone is holy and just. By His Word the heavens were created. By His Words were the stars flung into their places; the earth formed and the day separated from the night.

The Lord is not an idol: Eyes have they but they see not. Ears have they, but they hear not, neither are they attuned to the cries of the people. But the Lord sees His people; He is attuned to their voices and hears their calls. The Lord is nigh unto those that call upon His name; to those that call upon His name in righteousness and truth.

Bless the Lord, ye His people. Give glory to the One who hath created thee; to the One whose name is above every name.

Shout unto the Lord and give glory to Jesus for He hath bought thee with His own Blood and hath removed from thee the curse and bondage of sin. He hath freed thee by His Blood. He hath given unto thee eternal life through faith in His name.

The name of the Lord is a strong place; His name is a place of safety and security. In His name thou canst trust. In His name thou canst rest assured that He will do according to His righteous holiness and according to His Word.

The Lord is faithful; the Lord is holy in all His ways. He brings life to those dead in trespasses and sins. He brings joy to the downtrodden and peace to those in distress. The Lord Jesus is the source of life; for it is in Him that there is life and the life is the light of men.

The Lord brings to those that trust Him the Way of everlasting life and in Him is the fullness of joy. For the Lord Jesus is the Way, the Truth, and the Life; no one cometh to the Father but through Him.

Call upon the Lord and He will hear thee. Come to Jesus and He will guide thee in all thy ways; He will make for thee a straight path; a way into eternal life; a path of righteousness and holiness; a way that will lead thee to glory and into the Presence of the Holy Father, our God.

Give praise to the Lord for His goodness; sing praises for His care of thee. Bless the Lord and give glory unto His name; for the name of Jesus is a sure and constant Power. His name is for thee a safe house of security.

Glory and honor, dominion and power be unto the Lord and unto His Christ.

For He hath had compassion on His children; to those called by His name hath be given the adoption as sons.

God hath taken upon himself the form of a servant and was made in the likeness of men. And being found in fashion as a man He humbled himself and became obedient unto death; even the death of the cross. Wherefore He is highly exalted and hath been given a name that is above every name; that at the name of Jesus every knee shall bow and every tongue confess that Jesus Christ is Lord to the glory of God the Father.

Give praise to the Lord, give praise. Shout, dance, and be glad for the Lord hath made for thee an eternal home in His presence and hath brought thee nigh by the Blood of Christ.

Holy is the Lord and most holy is His glorious name.

Psalm 21

How long wilt thou be far from me, O Lord my God? How long wilt thou hold thyself away from my call?

I am beset and troubled. My heart faints within me and my spirit is in despair. The enemy of my soul breaks upon me as the waves of the seas upon the rocks.

How long, O God, how long wilt thou not hear me? How long must I cry before thee before thou hearest my cries; before thou tunest thine ear unto me and doth help me?

But I know whom I have believed and am persuaded that He is able to keep that which I have committed unto Him against that day.

My spirit may lag; my soul may be besieged; my heart downcast. But the Lord is my God. He is my righteousness and my shield. He is the light of my life and the salvation of my soul.

I will trust in the Lord no matter what betide. I will present before Him my praises and the adoration of my heart no matter how heavy be my heart.

For the Lord hears my cries; His ears are attuned to my supplications. I am never alone nor am I ever forsaken. For the Lord is an ever-present help in time of trouble; a sure place of safety when the enemy comes in like a flood. For the name of Jesus hath raised up a standard against him. The enemy is defeated. Christ hath conquered death, hell, and the grave.

I am never alone. I am never without my God.

I may oft times feel without thee; but thy Word hath promised that thou wouldst never leave me nor forsake me. Thy Word hath promised that neither death, nor life, nor angels, nor principalities, nor powers, nor things present, nor things to come, nor height, nor depth, nor any other creature, shall be able to separate us from the love of God, which is in Christ Jesus our Lord.

So though the enemy may rage; though he may try and bring to my heart despair and trouble, yet in the Lord will I put my trust. In Jesus will I put my faith and to Him will I give my heart, my soul, and my strength; for in His love I am founded; in His grace I am saved; in His faithfulness I am secure. The Lord Christ is my Rock; He is my safety in the times of trouble; He is my source of all good, all righteousness and all security.

So let the enemy rage. Let him blow about with his foul breath. For the Lord Jesus hath overcome. And in Him I too shall overcome by the Blood of the Lamb and by the word of my testimony.

Psalm 22

I am in need, O God. I am in need. I have no refuge but thee, O Lord my God, King of the Universe.

Heal me that I may be healed. Touch me with thy nail scarred hand and bring healing to my tortured body for I call upon thy Name of Lord Christ; hear me, I pray.

Breathe upon me with thy power. Cover me with thy wings that I may be in safety and be healed.

I have no one but thee. Thou art my God and my sustenance; my Lord, my Rock, my sure Deliverer.

My pain debilitates me. I am in sore need of thee, O thou my Comfort; O thou my Provider.

Hear me and touch me as I call upon thy name for thou art Yahweh-Rapha, the Lord that healeth me.

Thy wounds are a testimony to thy healing power for thy Word doth say that by thy stripes we are healed.

Come thou Healer; come and touch thy servant who calls upon thy name.

Thou hast sworn that thou wouldst give unto thy servants thine own power and in that power there is healing: Healing of the body; healing of the spirit; healing of the soul; healing of the emotions; yea, all healing is within thy hands by the power of thy Name.

I call upon thee, O Lord Jesus Christ; touch me and heal me. Bring to me thy power and touch my broken body for the glory of thy Name and for thy kingdom's power.

I praise thee, O Lord for thy touch. I praise thee, thou my Healer, for what thou wilt do in me. I give glory to thy name for thy Name is great. There is none like thee and I praise thee, O Lord, my Christ. Glory be to thy Name for ever and ever. Amen.

Psalm 23

Gracious unto me, art thou, O Lord, for I have called unto thee and thou hast heard me; yea, I called upon thy Name and thou didst come to my help.

My soul was sore within me. I didst nigh faint for pain of body and spirit, but thou, O Lord didst hear me out of thy holy temple and didst stretch forth thy nail scarred hand and didst bring me healing.

Thou hast heard me, O God, when I called upon thy Name and thou didst turn thine ear to my voice. Thy Name, Lord Jesus hast been my strong help.

When I laid in pain, I called upon thy Name; when my body did ache and my spirit was failing me I called, Lord help me, and thou didst hear me.

How can I praise thee enough for thy goodness to me O Lord my God, my King, my Sovereign? How can these poor lips of mine do justice to the glory due to thy greatness? For thou art God; there is none besides thee. It was thy voice that spun the planets into their orbits and scattered the stars in the universe as seed upon a plowed field. It was the words of thy mouth that caused the mountains to rise up and the seas to cover the earth.

Thy word, O God didst bring into being all that is and shall be, save man which thou didst create with thine own hand and in thine own image.

Glorious is this God who created. Majestic is this Lord who heals. Awesome is the name of the Lord Jesus Christ, who was and is, and is to come. Glory and honor, dominion and power be unto thy name both now and forevermore.

Thou art a God who hears. Thine ear is attuned to the calls of thy people. Thou dost not slumber, neither doth thou close thine eyes in rest; yea, He who keeps His people will neither slumber nor sleep. For the Lord cares for those who are called by His name; to those who have been bought with the price of His own blood the Lord doth turn His ear.

Thanks be to thee, O Lord for thy mercy; thy sure favor doth cover thy people as a hen doth cover her chicks with her wings; so doth the Lord cover His people; yea, He doth stretch forth His arms and doth enfold His own.

Psalm 24

How couldst there be a God that never had beginning and will never have an end?

How couldst there be a God that is perfect in all His aspects; omnipotent, omnipresent, and omniscient?

How couldst there be a God that chose to demonstrate Himself as the Father of all creation, who chose to take on human form and become as one of His own creations and who presents Himself to His people through the power of His Spirit?

How couldst He be everywhere at the same time?

How couldst He listen to everyone's prayers and give personal attention to each individual?

How couldst there be a God who is total in holiness?

How couldst there be a God that is love?

My mind cannot comprehend the totality of God. I question; I wonder; and I find no logic in my own mind to understand.

Yet, He is God. He hath told by His own Word that His thoughts are not like my thoughts and His ways are not like my ways.

He is God and God alone. There is none like Him. There is no other besides Him.

I do not understand all there is to understand about this God, yet, I believe in Him and I trust His Word. He is faithful and true. He is righteous and holy. He is gracious and merciful; He is loving and compassionate. He is gentle and kind.

He is my God and I bless His name.

I may not understand all there is no know about this God who has shown His love for me by dying and being my substitute, then rising again to life, and giving me victory over death, hell, and the grave.

I may not understand His never ending, yet, I understand His glory. I understand His majesty; His magnificence; His splendor and the grandeur of His Name.

I exalt Him because He is God. I praise Him because of His love for me. I adore Him for His closeness. I honor Him for His power.

I may not understand God but I am His; heart, soul, body, mind, and strength. All that is in me is His.

He is my God and I am His child. He loved me before I was formed in my mother's womb. He knew me before I came into this world. He loved me as He hung upon a cross dying for my sins; the sins I would not commit for nearly two thousand years future.

God is God no matter how my mind conceives of Him. God is God no matter what man may say about Him. God is God whether I fully understand Him or not. God is God. And this God that I worship, this God that I adore; this God that is my salvation and my strength; my hope and my eternal security; this God who is my Lord and my King and my refuge is mine and I am His.

There is no god like my God; there is none like Him! He alone is holy; He alone is glorious is all His being; He is precious to me because I was precious enough to Him that He loved me from the foundations of the earth.

The love of God is like water to a dying man. The love of God is like rain to the parched earth. The love of God is overwhelming yet personal and intimate and sure.

I may wonder about all the aspects of this God, yet, I give myself to Him. My mind may question about His being, yet, I do not doubt Him.

His power has been displayed in my life. His love has been shed abroad in my heart by His Holy Spirit.

God is my God and I will give Him glory for all of my life; for He is worthy of all my praise and all my worship; if He never does another thing for me; if I never feel His presence again; if I never sense His love and His mercy again; I will praise Him and I will always be His child, for He is God. Blessed be His name!

Psalm 25

This world is not my home. This place is but a stepping stone to my eternal destination in the Presence of the One who loved me and hath given His life that I might be with Him throughout all eternity.

My home is the Presence of the Lord my God; for thou hast prepared a place for me by thine own promise.

Thou hast said that where thou art there too shall I be because I trust in thee. Thou art faithful and true to thine own word and thy promises are yea and amen.

My soul longs for thy Presence, O my Lord Christ; my soul longs for thy Presence.

My faith reaches out for thy Kingdom; thy Throne is my dearest desire; to see thy face and to worship thee throughout all eternity.

There may be golden streets in the New Jerusalem and there may be gates of pearls. This city may be foursquare and the foundation may be gem strewn; but the face of my Lord Jesus is my destination; my desire; my hope and my eternal glory.

To see thee and worship thee; to bow before thee and praise thee; to give to thee my thanks and to see thy nail scarred hands is my hope and my destination.

I long for thy Presence, O God; I long for thy Presence.

Though I long for thee, O Lord, yet I pray, hold thou off coming, Lord, for there be too many who knoweth thee not neither hath they heard thy Word and the Gospel of thy peace.

Let the nations hear. Let the peoples come in contact with thy Gospel; the good news of the Lord Jesus Christ and His atonement for all sins.

Let the people of the earth be touched by thy Spirit; let thine anointing be spread throughout all the earth that thy Name might be glorified and thy Kingdom expanded.

I long to be with thee, O Lord my Savior; I long to be with thee.

The troubles of this world encompass me; the enemy of my soul besets me roundabout and doth fire his darts at my soul; yet will I trust in the Lord for if the Lord be for me who then shall stand against me?

Thy power doth abide in me by the Presence of thy Spirit; the Holy Ghost hath filled me and I am possessed by my God.

My soul cries, come thou Lord Jesus. My soul cries out to thee.

Come thou fount of every blessing. Come thou long awaited Jesus. Come and take thy people. For the Lord himself shall descend from heaven with a shout; with the voice of the archangel and with the trump of God; and the dead in Christ shall rise first, then those of us who remain shall be caught up together with them in the clouds to meet the Lord in the air; and so shall we ever be with the Lord. Wherefore comfort one another with these words.

Psalm 26

Teach me, Lord to be quiet. Teach me to know how to be still and wait for Thee.

Make quiet my spirit that I might hear Thee when thou dost speak to me.

I long to hear thy voice, O Lord; I long to hear thy voice.

The world surrounds me. So many voices and sounds and distractions take my ears.

Teach me, Lord, how to hear thee in the quiet places; in the silences of my devotion; in the stillness of my meditations; teach me to hear thee.

Thy fellowship, O my God is my joy. Thy Presence is the blessing of my days; the benediction to my nights.

To know Thee, to feel Thee, to sense the manifestation of Thee within me and around me is my deepest desire, O Lord, my Jesus, my Savior.

Teach me to be silent in my spirit, that Thy Spirit may come to me; that Thy glory may surround me; that the brilliance of thy Most Holy Spirit may fill me to overflowing and sanctify me fully.

Let my ears be attuned to the voice of Thy Spirit, O Lord my God. Let my ears be attuned to Thy voice.

Help me to blot out the sounds of the world around me; to ignore anything but Thy voice; Thy Words; Thy pronouncements to my soul.

Nothing is more to me than Thy Presence, O my Lord Christ; nothing is more to me than Thee.

Teach me, Lord, to know the still small voice that is Thine. Thou art not in the tempest; thou art not in the thunder; thou art not in the whirlwind. Thou art in the quiet places; the silence of my soul is where I find Thee.

My soul searcheth for Thee, O Lord my God; my heart calls out to the God of my salvation.

I peruse Thy Word; I study that which Thou hast spoken through the Prophets and Apostles; I survey the Scriptures and I find Thee there. But I long to hear Thy voice, O God of my heart. I long to hear Thee speak to me and show me that which is Thy will for me.

Thy will, O God, is where I long to be. Thy will is the place of my inner satisfaction and completion.

To Thee I call, O Jesus, my Lord. Teach me to listen. Teach me to be quiet and wait for Thee. Tutor me in lingering in silence; that in silence I may hear Thee; and in hearing Thee, bow to Thy will that in all my ways I may please Thee and Thy sanctification may complete me.

Psalm 27

Potter mold me; make me into thine own image Lord Christ; for Thou art the former of my life; the molder of my spirit.

I am thy clay, O my God; I am wetted upon thy wheel Great Fashioner of the earth.

As the planet was formed by the Word coming from the mouth of the Lord; as man was formed from the dust of the earth by the hand of God; so is my life being molded by my Savior; by His Spirit doth He shape me into the pattern of His own likeness.

I yield to the touch of thy hand, O my Potter; as the clay yields to the hands of he who forms it.

Thou art my God and I surrender to Thee; for Thy Will shall make of me what thou wilt; yea, I shall be even as my God doth please to make me.

For as the lamp gave no protest to the way it was formed, so am I to the will of my God.

I surrender all I am to thee, my God; to thy hand doth I commit all that is within me; yea, to Thy will doth I give all that I am, all I have been and all I will ever be; for Thou art my God: Thou art my Jesus, my Savior, my Lord.

In times past I walked in my own way; I did that which was good in mine own eyes; but the Lord took hold of me and His Spirit sanctified my innermost being and I became a new man in Christ Jesus my Lord.

Sanctify me wholly, O Lord my God; Great Spirit majestic, sanctify thou me.

Let nothing be left behind of the old man; purge me of all I was that I might be all that Thou wouldst have.

As the old Adam in me was dispelled by Thy Blood, Lord Jesus, so shall the new Adam be displayed in me by Thy sanctifying power.

Cleanse me, O God that I may be clean; sanctify me that I may be holy unto Thee.

Clothe me in the white robes of Thine own righteousness, O Potter of that which was shattered: Thou hast taken the broken pieces of my life and hath molded me into a new vessel; a vessel of praise shall I be unto my God: to the Lord Jesus Christ of Nazareth shall I bring forth the praises of my life.

Mold me, O God; form in me Thine Image that the world may see Jesus in me and that Thy Kingdom may be exalted.

Blessed be the hands of the Potter who forms from naught and maketh vessels of honor to His name.

Glorious shall be that vessel that the Lord uses to His praise.

Psalm 28

The eyes of the world look towards thy holy City, O God, the City of David; the Mount of Zion.

Peace, peace they say, let there be peace.

But the hosts of the earth neglect thy holy places, O God; they look towards Jerusalem and speak of peace but no peace comes.

Neither shall there be peace in the holy places of Zion until Yeshua HaMessiach, Jesus the Christ, shall return and set up His Kingdom upon the earth and shall reign in justice and righteousness from the New Jerusalem.

Thou, O Christ, art peace. Thou art solace in a storm; thou art rest in weariness and joy in mourning. But aside from Thee there is no peace, neither shall Zion be at rest until Thy foot shall again stand upon the Mount of Olives and Thy Kingdom come to the nations of the earth.

Thy prophet hath said, pray for the peace of Jerusalem, and so my prayer doth go up before Thee, thou that dwellest on High.

Let Jerusalem say, the Lord reigns. Let the daughters of Zion sing praises to He who is sovereign in all the earth. Sing to the Lord ye daughters of Zion; shout to the Lord for thy King cometh unto thee, the King of Glory.

Who is this King of Glory? Yahweh strong and mighty, Yahweh, mighty in battle, He is the King of Glory. Yet thy Word doth say that we crucified the king of glory. Jesus is the one strong and mighty. It is He who did battle against the evil one and against death, hell, and the grave and hath arisen victorious and shall reign forever and ever, even in Zion of city of the great King; for Yahweh has become salvation. Yeshua.

Peace be upon Jerusalem when she shall see the Righteous One coming in His glory. Peace be upon the people of the Book and let them bring praises to the name of He who is glorious in victory; to Jesus the Messiah, the Christ.

Psalm 29

Thy blood, O Jesus my God, thy blood doth plead for me. Thy blood hath been shed that I might inherit eternal life, yet it doth provide for me a way into thy throne room, O God my Savior.

Thy blood doth make the demons tremble and darkness flees when Thy blood is applied.

How wide reaching, how strong, how eternal, and how efficacious is the blood flowing from the wounds of my Lord?

Thy blood doth save, Thy blood doth cleanse, and Thy blood doth eradicate the stains of the taint of Adam upon me.

Thy blood shall never lose its power for Thou art forever glorified; Thou hast conquered and released thy servants from the bondage of the Egypt of sin that is within us.

The Lamb hath been slain. Propitiation is made; the price of paid; death is vanquished. Praise be to the name of the Lamb of God, Jesus Christ the Righteous.

For without the shedding of blood there is no remission of sin, and Thou, O Lord, didst become a little lower than the angels for the suffering of death, as the perfect Lamb that thou mightiest become the Lion of Judah.

What brought Thee, O Lamb to become a man? Why didst thou leave thy holy Throne to suffer the agony of being a man and dying upon the cross? Why hast thou given thyself, O Righteous One who hath no mark of sin upon or within thee?

Because of love thou didst come. Because of love thou didst become obedient unto death, even the death of the cross; wherefore God hath highly exalted Thee and given Thee a name that is above all names that at the name of Jesus, every knee shall bow and every tongue confess that Jesus Christ is Lord, to the glory of God the Father.

Thou art alpha and omega, Thou art alef and bet, the First and the Last, the Beginning and the End, and Thou art blessed forevermore. Amen.

Psalm 30

Thy brilliance doth dazzle me, O thou Most High. The glory of Thy Presence doth thrill my soul.

Thou hast flung the stars into space and hath created the universe by thy Word. There is nothing that is that Thou, O Lord hath not created; all that exists is by the imagining of Thy mind and the breath of Thy mouth.

Thou hast formed the earth and hath separated the dry land from the waters. Thou hast created sun and moon, yea, the clouds are thine and the winds blow by Thy command.

The mountains sprang forth and the rivers did flow by Thy Word; Forests covered the hills and deserts the wastelands.

The planets doth orbit by Thy command, yea by Thy Word doth they spin in their circles.

Thy voice is heard in the thunder and the earth quakes at the step of Thy foot. The heavens are Thy throne room and the earth is Thy footstool.

Thou dost ride upon the winds and the mountains rise up and give Thee praise for Thy greatness, O Lord.

The trees clap their hands and the rivers give voice to Thy glory.

Thou art great, O Lord God of Hosts; thou who art the champion of all the Hosts of Heaven; Jesus is Thy name and all creation doth rise to praise Thee, O Lord, for thou hast formed all things by Thy Word and with thine own hand hast Thou formed man from the dust of the earth and hast breathed into man the breath of lives that man might become a living soul.

Holy art thou, O thou Creator of all; blessed is Thy name forevermore.

Sun and moon, stars and comets, planets and all celestial hosts give praise to the Lord for He is great; His name is awesome before all creation, yea, His praise is echoed in the whirlwind and blasted by the waves upon the rocks of the sea.

Praise be to Thee, O thou whose Word hath made all and by whose Presence all is kept in order. Blessed is the Lord Jesus Christ; glory and honor, dominion and power be unto thee O great God of gods.

Psalm 31

Praise the Lord for His goodness and His mercy.
Praise the Lord for His grace and His understanding.
Praise the Lord for His peace and His Presence.
Praise the Lord for His salvation and His Spirit.
Praise the Lord for His cross and His empty tomb.
Praise the Lord for His power and His might.
Praise the Lord for keeping His people in righteousness.
Praise the Lord for His protection and His guidance.
Praise the Lord, ye His people. Praise the Lord all His saints.
Let the redeemed of the Lord give praise unto His name; to His majestic name let all the blood-bought give praise.
Praise the Lord for His forgiveness and His benevolence.
Praise the Lord for His rule and His majesty.
Praise the Lord for His dominance and His control.
Praise the Lord for His defense and His security.
Praise the Lord for His glory and His splendor.
Praise Him for His beauty and His grandeur.
Praise Him for His triumph. Praise Him for His victory.
Praise the Lord all the earth; let all that exists by the Word of the mouth of our God give praise to His holy name forever and ever.
Praise ye the Lord.

Psalm 32

Give me the heart of a servant, O thou Lord my God. Grant unto thy Blood-bought son the heart of a servant that I might be unto thy Kingdom an example of Thee.

Thou wert a servant, Lord, though Thou wast God in the flesh, yet didst thou serve thine own creation; and by thy service didst thou become obedient unto death, even the death of the cross.

Give me the heart if a servant, O Lord, that I might show forth thy glory to the nations and thy power to those that believe not in thee.

Take out this heart of flesh and give me the heart of a servant; a heart like unto thy heart that in me thou mayest be glorified and thy holy name exalted.

Create in me a clean heart, O God and remove from me all sense of self and personal desire that I may be thy true servant and a servant to those that thou wilt send me; those that hear of thee through my voice, let me be a bondsman to thy children.

O Lord my God, O Jesus my Redeemer, remove from me all sense of self and let me in all ways rely on thy Spirit and Thy power that I might show forth thy glory in all the earth and proclaim thy Gospel in Thy power and Thy might in humble servitude and meekness.

O heart within me, be thou gone and let the Spirit of Almighty God create within me the new heart of a servant that I may be as the Lord my God wouldst have me and let me, in humbleness show forth of power of the Holy Ghost that abideth in me.

Be thou glorified, O Jesus by the heart of a servant within me that thy name and thy Kingdom may be exalted and all honor may be thine.

Psalm 33

Come to me thou Spirit of the Almighty One. Renew within me thy Presence.

My soul is dry; my heart is parched. I am in need of thee, O Thou Water of Life.

Come to me and delay not, O God. My soul thirsts for thee as in a dry and baron land; as in a desert seeking an oasis, I long for the quenching of Living Water.

Come, Holy Spirit, I need thee. Come sweet Spirit, I pray. Come in thy strength and thy fullness. Come in thine own special way.

Come thou Almighty King; come reviving Spirit.

Fill me to overflowing with Thy Presence, O God. Fill me that I may be complete in thee. Consume me that I may be lost in thy Presence.

Apart from Thee, O Lord, I am undone and lost. Without the Spirit of Christ, I am nothing.

Hear my call, O God. Turn thine ear to me Lord Jesus and come to me. Fill me with Thy Presence; thy person; thy fullness.

Let self be consumed by thy radiance, O thou Most High. Take from me my selfish nature; all that displeaseth Thee let it be consumed by Thy Spirit.

Take me; melt me; mold me; use me.

Fall fresh on me, O God; Descend on me, Spirit Most Holy.

Let Thy power fall on me; let me be filled with Thee that I may be full.

I need Thee, Lord; I need Thee.

Pour forth on me thine anointing, O God; let the oil of thy Spirit be poured forth upon me.

Spirit of God, come upon me in thy power and thy Presence. Show forth in me thy glory. Shine forth through me Thy radiance.

Spirit Most Holy, God Most High, Lord Jesus, my Savior, anoint thou thy servant; fill me Spirit of God.

Psalm 34

Holy is the Lord and worthy of glory; who spoke and the worlds were formed.

Holy is the Lord and glorious in all His aspects; who by His strong right arm lead Israel out of bondage and into a new land.

Holy is the Lord and marvelous to His people; who forgives repented sins and grants grace to all who ask of Him.

Holy is the Lord and righteous in all His ways; who took upon Himself the form of a servant and was made in the likeness of men.

Holy is the Lord and holy is His name; who became obedient unto death; even the death of the cross.

Holy is the Lord and wonderful in majesty; who has been given a name that is above every name, that at the name of Jesus every knee shall bow and every tongue confess that Jesus Christ is Lord, to the glory of God the Father.

Holy is the Lord and splendid in His mercy; who has shed abroad in our hearts His love by the Holy Ghost.

Holy is the Lord and celebrated is His reign; who was and is and is to come. The Lord of Hosts is He.

Holy is the Lord and blessed is His nature; who loves the unlovable and gives grace to the unworthy.

Holy is the Lord and great is He above all gods; who has shown His love to the world through the Lord Jesus and has given salvation through His name.

Holy is the Lord and marvelous in the heavens; who orders all things by the word of His power and knoweth all things within Himself.

Holy is the Lord and virtuous is He; who shows wonders in the heavens and His power in the lives of the Blood-bought.

Holy is the Lord and powerful beyond understanding; who is worshipped by all the Hosts of Heaven; to whom the seraphim give praise.

Holy is the Lord and holy is His name; who gives joy to the upright and brings the sinful down to the pit.

Holy is the Lord and brilliant in His power; who reigns in glory forever and ever.

Holy is the Lord and hallowed is His name; who sets apart the Blood-washed and anoints them with His Spirit.

Holy is the Lord and awesome in His holiness; who sends forth His Spirit into the hearts of those who have been washed in Jesus' blood.

Holy is the Lord and worthy of all glory. Holy is the Lord. Amen.

Psalm 35

My soul is like a desert; how hast thou come to be so dry, O my soul?

Like a parched and wasted land, so is my spirit within me, for I long for the Presence of my God; yea, I thirst for the living water of the Spirit of the Lord.

As a man longing for streams in the desert so doth my soul long for the refreshment of the Spirit of my God.

How long shall I wander in the wilderness of desolation? How long shall I feel the misery of needing Thee, O my Lord Christ?

Come to me, O God, refresh and satisfy this longing of my soul.

I call unto Thee, O Lord, hear my plea. Leave me not in need of thine anointing; the water of Thy Presence satisfying and thrilling my soul with Thy nearness.

O my God, I need Thee. Come Spirit of Jesus and wash over me.

Bring me back to the land of milk and honey; to the promised land of thy Presence.

Without Thee I am wasted; I am undone and longing; my soul pants for Thee as a hart for the clear water of a brook.

My feet shuffle along the pathway of my life not knowing where I am headed or what is lying ahead of me in the distance.

The dust of life surrounds me; with the sands of this valley, I struggle lest they cover me.

Bring me to the water of Thy Presence, O Lord my God, my Savior, my Rock.

As thou didst bring water from the rock in the wilderness, bring forth Thy Water in me, O Lord; fountain of the Holy Ghost whelm up in me.

Do not let my steps continue without Thy guidance, O Jesus, my God. Let the richness of Thy Presence come to me; bring the enlightenment of thy Spirit and show me the way that I am to trod.

My confidence is in Thee, O Lord; thou shalt direct my path.

Revive me, Lord Jesus. Bring back life to these dry bones. Thou hast promised to return that which the cankerworm hath eaten and I trust in Thee, O Jesus, my God. Revive thou me, O God, that in the wealth of thy Presence I may be revived, renewed and revitalized, and this dry valley be turned into a land bursting forth with the power and Presence of thy Holy Spirit. Revive me, O God. Revive thou me.

Psalm 36

Song of my soul, let me sing the praises of the Lord Most High; the God of greatness and might; of mercy and justice; of understanding and knowledge.

Song of my soul, let glory spring forth from my lips; the praises that whelm up within me as a spring in an oasis.

Song of my soul, give acclaim to the One God of Heaven; sing and give laud to the Creator of all.

Song of my soul, pay tribute to the King of Glory; the Lord Christ who bought thee with a price and hath given unto thee eternal life by his own death and resurrection.

Song of my soul, resound the majesty of He who reigns.

Let the joy of my soul break forth in song. Let the song, that is the Spirit within me, give praise to He who is worthy of all praise.

Song of my soul, Thou art Jesus my Lord; Thou art the one who gives song to my spirit and delight to my being.

O Jesus, I praise thee. I lift up my heart before thee and give honor and glory unto thy most holy name.

Thou art my song, my melody and the harmony of Thy Presence within me.

Song of my soul, sing praises; sing praises unto the Lord my God while I have any being; while life is within me let me sing the song of the redeemed.

Psalm 37

Dawn maker, great Lord God of Hosts, holy is thy name and blessed art thou forever and ever.

Thou who doth paint the glory of sunrise, praise be to thy name.

Thou who has blended the colors of a sunset, glory to Thee.

The Lord is the Artist of Glory who hath given a blessing to mankind in the beauty He hath placed throughout His creation.

Holy Lord, thou glorious Painter, my lips shall ever speak thy praise; my heart shall ever bow before thee in worship.

Thou art glorious, O Lord. Thy name is to be praise from the rising of the sun to the going down of the same.

Day by day I witness thy loving-kindness and thy tender mercies which are ever before mine eyes in thy creation.

When I rise in the morning my heart goes out to thee, O Jesus, my God.

When I lay me down to rest, thou Lord, art in my heart and in my mind and thy worship shall spill forth from me as a stream in a desert.

How glorious is the Lord God of Heaven; how awesome is His Presence?

For the Lord made the heavens and the earth. By His own words hath He formed all that exists.

So to the Lord of Glory, the Father of our great God and Savior, Jesus Christ, be all praise, glory, adoration, exaltation, and rejoicing.

Blessed is thy name O Lord, my God. Holy art thou, O thou that doth rule the Universe.

Thy glory is seen in the sunrise, thy majesty in the setting of the sun. In the coolness of moonlight and in the sparkling of the stars is the name of our God exalted.

Praise be to thee, O thou Painter of Creation and praise to thy most holy name.

Psalm 38

The Lord rises in glory, may His name be praised.

The Lord rules in righteousness, may His name be exalted.

The Lord doth show His love to all, may He ever be honored and adored.

The Lord shines His glory upon His creation, may His name be raised high.

The Lord is good to all, may His name be glorified.

The Lord is faithful in all His ways, may His glory shine from the heavens.

The Lord is holy and just, may His name be acclaimed.

The Lord is One, may His name be held in honor.

The Lord displays His power, may His name be glorified.

The Lord is the King of the Universe, may He ever be adored.

The Lord hath provided salvation, may the name of Jesus be worshipped.

The Lord is just, may His name be given great thanksgiving.

The Lord is the light of the world, may His name be ever praised.

Blessed be the Lord God of Hosts and blessed is His most holy name forever.

Psalm 39

Spirit of the Most High, burn in me; bright fire of the glory, flame up within me.

Rise up, O God, and kindle within me a new and brilliant blaze that thy Spirit might be strong in me and thy holiness spread throughout my soul.

Shine forth, O Spirit of God; let the conflagration of thy glory spread an inferno in me.

O Lord, my Lord, I thirst for Thee. My soul doth long for thy Presence and the dryness within me is ready for thy combustion.

Burn within me O Lord; For as the prophet Jeremiah hath said, his word was in mine heart as a burning fire shut up in my bones.

My heart is kindling, O Lord Christ; the dry sticks of my life and the brushwood of my soul are ready for the spark of divine fire that is Thy Presence and Thy glory through Thy Spirit, O most High.

Come, Holy Spirit, and sear away all the dross of my most wicked self. Mold in me the image of thine own Presence, Lord Jesus, my Savior and my God.

Create in me, O God, a clean heart. Burn away all that displeaseth thee that remaineth of mine old self and make me like Thee.

Image of Christ shine forth in me as daybreak. Shatter all that is unrighteous within me and make me pure before thee.

As gold is refined in the fire and all dross is burned away, so Lord make me as gold; even as pure fine gold.

Reduce to ashes all of self and remake me in thine image. Jesus shine forth in me. Lord Christ let the glory of thy brilliance and the radiance of thy Spirit be within me and animate me by thy power.

Infuse me with thy strength. Arouse in me a fire that is unquenchable.

Spirit of the living God, flow throughout my being. Consume me. Engulf me. Tear down all the idols of my own idolatry that is my self. Create in me the image of Jesus that I may be like Thee and in all my ways please thee and shine forth thy glory and thy love to the world.

Spirit of the Most High burn in me.

Psalm 40

Speak thou to my heart, O God of my salvation. Speak unto my soul thy will that I may follow Thee and do according as thou dost lead.

I am thy servant, Lord God of Hosts. I bow before thee for thou art my Lord and my God and there is none beside thee, nor shall there ever be.

Speak thou to thy servant, O my Master; give me thy guidance that I may do thy will.

I have erred in times past and have done according to mine own desires, even though I didst think I was following thee, yet I found myself out of thy will.

Let me 'nere be outside of thy holy pleasure and thy will.

Let me 'nere think that mine own mind can discern what is right, or just or holy, or what is thy will for my life.

O Lord, my God, my Lord Jesus, my Master and my Sovereign, let me follow only thy Spirit and thy will.

Speak Lord for thy servant is listening. Speak, O God, that I might do thy will.

I long to follow thee, O Lord, Supreme Ruler of all Creation.

Spirit of God, take hold of my life. Spirit, Most High, consume thy servant.

Let me not walk according to mine own mind but let me follow only thee and thy will.

I am thy servant, Lord Jesus, use me as thou wouldst. Speak and I will follow thee.

Psalm 41

I praise thee, O Lord my God for thou art the Lord of my life; my strength and my sure hope and salvation.

Thou O Lord, hath loved me with an everlasting love.

Though I am a sinful man, full of selfishness and deceit, yet Thou hast loved me and sacrificed thyself for me.

Thou didst leave thy Throne and thy heavenly Kingdom to come and live as one of thine own creation; as a man, that thou couldst redeem mankind by thine own Blood.

How I praise thee, O Lord for thy goodness; how I glorify thee for thy power.

Thou art a great and wondrous God full of mercy and compassion.

Thy loving-kindness is better than life.

Thou hast bought me with thine own Blood and thou hast sanctified thy servant by thy Spirit.

Make of thy servant a useful vessel, O Lord God of Hosts. Make me, mold me, fill me, and use me, O thou great Creator of all things.

Take away anything within me that displeaseth thee, O Lord. Open my heart that it may become thy Throne, O God.

Create in me a clean heart. Make my life a tabernacle for thy Spirit.

May I be clothed with thine own righteousness O God. Wrap me within the white robes of thy righteousness that I may be pure. Take away all mine iniquity O God and purge me of anything that displeaseth thee.

Use me as thy voice O God. May my words be thine that thou mayest be glorified by my life.

Raise me up as thy servant that I may abase myself before thee and that thou mayest shine through me for thine own glory.

I praise thee O God. Lord Jesus, I exalt thee.

Thou and thou alone art the Lord of my life and unto thee, O Lord Christ do I bow my heart and my knees.

Accept my worship, O God that it may be pleasing to thee and that the name of Jesus Christ of Nazareth may be exalted throughout the earth.

Psalm 42

Lord, help me! I want to do thy will. My desire is to thee, O God, and my soul longs for thy Presence.

Keep myself from being in thy path, Lord Jesus. Help me to know thy will and do it and help me keep mine own desires and mine own will away from the course that thou dost set for me.

Father, I am a needy man. I am sinful and undone, willful and my nature is against thee. But thou hast given me of thy Spirit, O Lord my God and thou hast created in me a new heart. Thou hast replaced my heart of stone with a heart of flesh and my desire is towards thee.

Be thou my strong tower, Lord; let me run unto thee and be safe.

Help me, Lord, to give over all I am to thy Spirit's power. Take all the secret kingdoms of my heart and break them apart. Take all of me and make me thy true and willing servant. Break apart my willfulness and my self-desire and replace it with thy Spirit.

Be thou strong in me O God that I may serve thee. Take all of me and make me a tabernacle of thy Spirit that thou mayest reside in me in righteousness and holiness and that I may be thine own in all things.

Holy One I bless thy name for thou art my God and I praise thee; thou art my Lord and I worship the name of my Lord Jesus Christ.

I give thee my thanks, O Lord, for the comfort and Presence that I know thou hast given me. Blessed is thy name O Lord forever and ever.

Psalm 43

Early in the morning my voice is raised to the Lord of Host, my God. I rise contemplating the wonders of the Lord; His praise is on my lips as the sun rises.

Glory and honor are thine, O Lord. Great and mighty art thou.

When I rise I will praise the Lord. I will give to God honor and praise; the adoration of my heart.

Majestic in holiness is the Lord God Almighty; who was and is and is to come; the Sovereign Lord; the matchless King.

Great and mighty is the Glorious One of Heaven.

While I live will I give praise to the Lord Jesus; while breath is in my body I will exalt His holy name.

At midday I will sing praises to the Lord. When the sun rides high in the sky I will praise Jesus' name; for He is great and awesome in majesty; glorious in all His ways and blessed in His love for his children. He is a matchless King; a magnificent God is the Lord Jesus Christ.

My soul exalts the Lord; my mouth will sing the praises of my God. Wonderful is thy name Lord Jesus and splendid is thy majesty in all the earth.

At nighttime I will lift up my hands and praise the Lord. I will raise my voice to the Lord of my life. For thou hast brought me out of the pits of despair and brought me into thy Kingdom and hath clothed me in the white robes of thine own righteousness that I may live with thee forever.

Praise to the Lord of Hosts is the cry of my heart.

As the darkness covers the earth the Light of Life shines forth within me and I will forever praise the Lord.

Psalm 44

How glorious is the Lord my God; how majestic is His Presence. When I wake in the mornings, behold, Lord, thou art there. Thou hast wrapped me in thy goodness and surrounded me with thy grace. Thy love hath been shed abroad in my heart by the Holy Ghost and my soul bows before Thy holiness and doth bless thy name.

Thy name, Lord Jesus, is power. There is none greater than thee. Thou hast conquered death, hell and the grave and hath made the enemy of my soul a defeated foe, a vanquished adversary, a beaten opponent. Though he may seek those that he may devour thy sacrifice hath made him as defeated. Though he may roar as a lion yet someday even his knee shall bow and his tongue confess that Jesus Christ is Lord to the glory of God the Father. How magnificent is that name O Lord. Thou art a God of power and might. All that thou hast created gives praise to thee for thou and thou alone art God.

Thy praise, O Lord shall be my war cry. Thy glory shall be my battle banner; For thou art Jehovah Nissi.

When the enemy shall come in like a flood the Lord shall raise up a standard against him. Thy cross Lord Jesus is my standard. I shall ever bear it before me as an ensign that the enemy may see and tremble as the Saints of the Most High tear down his kingdom and shall lay it at the feet of Jesus proclaiming the Lord Christ as Lord of All, King of all kings and glorious God of all gods.

My worship shall flow unto thee O God as a river doth flow to the sea. My praise shall ever rise to thee as incense; yea, as sweet incense shall the praises of thy Saints ascend to thy Throne and shall mingle with the cries of the seraphim.

The Lord of Hosts is glorious. He is the King of Glory. Yet thy Word doth say that they crucified the Lord of glory. But thou didst not stay in the grave, neither didst death keep hold on thee for thy power is greater than death, far superior to the grave and thou didst rise to life though thou hath been dead. Now liveth the Lord Christ. Jesus is alive and His Saints bless His name. The Blood-bought doth glory in the Lord their God and the praises of the Most High shall ever be on the lips of thy people, O Lord.

Holy is the Lord and majestic is His name.

Blessed is the Lord and His people shall make His name glorious.

Thou art great, O Lord, and greatly to be praised.

The heavens declare the glory of God and the firmament showeth His handiwork. All that exists doth give praise to the Lord for He and He alone is God. There is none like our God.

Rise up ye Saints of the Lord. Rise up and give praise to the matchless One. Rise up and praise His name. Shout His glories to the heavens and declare His wonders among the peoples of the earth.

There is none like our God. There is none like the Lord of Hosts. The Almighty One is a God alone; there is none like Him neither shall there ever be another. He and He alone is God. Jesus is His name and His people bow in reverence before Him and shall cast their crowns at His feet. Jesus is Lord; King of kings is He. Blessed be His name now and forever.

Psalm 45

Risen and glorious; Alive and victorious; Living forever is the Lord Jesus Christ. The Lord hath come forth from the grave and hath conquered death and hell.

All praise to you, Lord Jesus; for thou alone wert dead and now art alive. Thou alone hath shaken off the dread, cold chains of death and hath emerged to life again and hath been glorified forever. Praised be thy name, O Lord.

Thou didst hang on the cross of Calvary. Thou didst suffer agony and torment beyond the understanding of man. Thou wert spit upon and beaten, maligned and crowned with thorns. Thou didst have stripes upon thy back and those stripes have brought healing to thy Body, the Church.

Thine obedience hath taken thee to the cross and because thou wert obedient unto death, yea, even the death of the cross, God hath highly exalted thee and hast given thee a name that is above every name, that at the name of Jesus, every knee shall bow and every tongue confess that Jesus Christ is Lord to the glory of God the Father; wherefore I praise thee O Lord for thy obedience and thine acceptance of the sentence of death for the sins of the world.

Thou art glorious, O Lord, Jesus the Christ and thy name shall forever be praised.

As thou art extolled now in Heaven so shalt thou, at that day, be praised throughout all the earth. Thou shalt be King over all and thy Lordship shall be forever and forever.

Glory and honor is thine O Lord. Glory and honor, dominion and power be unto the Lord Christ both now and forever.

Rise up, ye Blood-bought and proclaim the King of kings. Shout for joy to the Lord Christ for He is alive forevermore.

His dominion shall not end and His sovereignty shall be forever.

Give praise to the wondrous One; give praise to the Lord of Hosts, the Lord Jesus Christ who is, and was and is to come.

Give praise to His name and honor to His majesty.

Shout and dance and glorify the Lord Jesus. Give praise to His name and honor to His eternal Godhead. Blessings and honor, glory and power be unto the Lord both now and forever. Praise the name of Jesus.

Psalm 46

Look to the skies ye people of the earth. Look and behold the wonders of thy God.

Gaze upon the mountains; the heights covered with pine and aspen, maples and oaks. Gaze upon the beauty displayed in the peaks, the rocks and crags for they display before thee the works of the hands of God.

For God hath spoken and He hath made; His voice went out into darkness and behold, light sprang from His words. He separated the light from the darkness and called forth the sun, moon, and stars; the sun to rule the day and the moon and stars to shine forth His glory in the nighttime.

Behold the wonders the Lord hath been set before thee, O man. Behold the majesty of the Holy One within all of what He hath called forth from nothing by His Word.

His Word went out all that is came into existence.

He spoken and creation happened.

All that exists came forth from the voice of Him who sits upon the Throne of Glory; the Lord strong and mighty; the Lord of Hosts, God of all.

Heaven and earth, angels and hosts, skies and glorious wonders, earth and all its beauty, man and his frailty, beasts of the field and all creeping thing, birds and animals, heights and depths, oceans and seas; all that is came forth from the Word of God.

Yet with all the wonders of creation displayed in the very eyes of man, he sees not the workings of the Lord; he understands not that God hath made him.

But God did not speak man into existence. He formed him from the dust of the earth and breathed into him the breath of lives and man became a living soul.

But though God didst fellowship with the first man, man chose against God and His commandments and did eat of the forbidden fruit, the fruit of the tree of the knowledge of good and evil, and so sin entered into the creation of God and separated man from His Creator.

But God so loved the world that He gave His only begotten Son that whosoever believeth in Him shall not perish but have everlasting life.

God loved the host of mankind He had created. He loved them so much that again His Word created. And the Word became flesh and dwelt among us and we beheld His glory; the glory as of the only begotten of the Father, full of grace and Truth.

Jesus, the Word of God incarnate hath provided salvation by His Blood. His life gave life to those of mankind who repent and turn to the Risen One as Savior.

Glory and honor, dominion and power are thine, O God, and thy people praise thee. Thou art Lord of all and we cry holy is the Lord of Hosts, God of Creation. Blessed art thou in all the universe, Lord God Almighty.

Psalm 47

O my God, Ancient of Days, Lord of heaven and earth, Father of my Lord Jesus Christ, hear the voice of thy servant. Hear me, O God, intune thine ear unto my call.

Come, Spirit of the Almighty One and infuse me with thy power.

I am weak and prone to mine own way but I call upon thee, O Lord, for thy Presence and thy power.

Work in me as thou wilt, O God. Shape me and make me according to thy will.

Do as thou wilt with me, O Lord and make thy servant a useful vessel, full of thy power and able to do that which thou hast set before me.

Let my heart be thy Throne, O God, my Savior; rule and reign in me.

Take me, Lord, as a potter doth take the clay and mold me into thine own image. Form within me the true image of the Lord Jesus. Let me live as He lived, walk as He walked, teach as He taught, think as His thoughts were always of thy will and thy Word. Form this imageless clay into a useful vessel. Make me into a vessel of honor and righteousness for thy name's sake.

Form me and mold me, make me and sculpt me into the likeness of the Lord Jesus.

Spirit of the Most High, pour into this vessel your holiness and your Presence. Let me be nothing but thine, O Lord.

Drench me in thy Presence; cover me and surround me with thy self that I might be thy true and useful servant.

Pour into me thy power, O God, that I might pour forth to the world thy Word, thy Presence, and thy glory and that all may see that Jesus Christ is Lord, to the glory of God the Father.

Take from me all that displeaseth thee, O Lord. Remove from me all sense of self and mine own interests and let me see only Jesus and His glory.

Create in me a clean heart, O God, that I may be thy servant and that thy Kingdom may be increased and thy glory displayed.

O Lord my God, change all of this sinful man into a useful container of thy Spirit and thy Presence. Remove from me all the stains of sin by the Blood of the Crucified One, who was dead but rose from the dead to life everlasting.

Change all of me by thy power, O God. Move in me and transform me. Revolutionize this clay into thine image, O Lord my God. Make me new and wholly thine.

Work in me thy will, O Lord. Take me as I am and renovate me by thy power. Take this sinful man and make me new by thy power and in the name of Jesus.

O Lord, my Savior, remove from me anything that stands in the way of thy will. Take from me all that hinders and doth thwart thy working in me. Take my will and conform it to thine, O God. Take thy servant and fill him with thy Presence; let me see thee and thee alone, O Lord my God. Let mine eyes be opened to see thee, O God. Show me thy glory and let me see thee as thou art.

Open the floodgates of heaven, O Lord, and pour out on me thy powerful blessings.

Take me and use me. Fill me and overwhelm me. Do as thou wilt with me, O Lord, that I may show Jesus to the nations; that the peoples of the earth may see in me the image of the Risen One and come to thee and thy Kingdom.

Spirit of God, hear me. Hear me and work in me. Change me and conform me to thine image.

Thou hast promised that from my belly would flow rivers of living water and this thou didst speak of the Holy Ghost for He was not yet given at that time. But now, O God, the time hath been fulfilled and thy Spirit hath been poured out upon thy people. Let that river of the Holy Ghost flow from me, O Lord.

Emanate from me, O Most Holy Spirit. Arise and emerge from me in a torrent of thy living water.

Open heaven and pour out thy Presence. Shine forth in me the light of thy glory that I may reflect thy brilliance and show forth thy power.

Hear the voice of my supplications, O God. Hear me and work thy most perfect will in me. Do what only thou canst do, O Ancient of Days, majestic Lord of all. Make me, mold me, fill me, and use me, O Lord Jesus, that thou mayest receive the glory and honor and that thy Kingdom may be increased and thy power displayed.

Hear me, O Lord my God. Hear me and do.

Psalm 48

Upon the mountain of the Lord wilt thou stand, O thou Risen One, thou Christ. Upon the Mount of Olives shalt thou stand and behold the nations shall come to thee and hail thee. The gatherings of the earth shall come forth and proclaim the sovereignty of the Lord Jesus.

Thou didst, as God, speak the universe into existence. Thou didst take upon thyself the form of a servant, a body like unto the body that thy hands did form from the dust of the earth, and thou didst sacrifice that body to torture, mocking and death.

Behold thou wast dead but lo, the grave could not hold thee and thou didst come forth in victory and didst conquer death, hell, and the grave by thy resurrection.

Heaven didst receive thee back and thou hast been standing at the right hand of the Majesty on High interceding for the saints.

How can my soul not bless the Lord for His salvation and His Spirit? How can I keep from shouting forth the majesty of my God?

The Lord shall be praised by my lips for He hath redeemed me from death, yea, He hath given me eternal life through Jesus Christ my Lord.

Raise up thy voice, O ye church of God, and give glory to the Lord Jesus who lives and reigns in majesty and power.

Lift up thy voices ye daughters of the saints and break forth in dancing for the Lord thy God is with thee, yea, He doth inhabit thee by His Spirit.

Raise up thy head ye gray beards and glorify the Lord of Heaven.

Shout for joy ye young ones and cry forth the praise of He who sits in majesty, even He who is from everlasting to everlasting, the Lord God of Hosts.

Come ye nations and behold the power of the Lord.

The mountains shall break forth in singing and the trees of the land shall clap their hands for the Lord is God over all the earth and creation doth show forth His glory.

The lion shall roar, and the lamb shall bleat. The eagle shall cry forth praise and the power of the horse shall be only as the voice of the Lord doth give them strength.

All creation praises the Lord God of Host, the Ancient of Days, the Almighty One. He alone is worthy of praise. It hath been by His voice that all things were called into existence. All the universe shows the glory of the Lord and by the Word of the Living Jesus hath all things come forth.

The nations shall witness thy glory when thou dost return, O Lord Christ; all the kings of the earth shall glorify thy name when thou art revealed in thy glory.

Praise the name of Jesus O peoples of the earth. Give glory to His name O ye Blood-bought!

Psalm 49

Are the heavens brass? Doth my voice and my supplications not reach to the Throne?

My soul longs for my God; yea, my heart thirsts for the Presence of my Lord and Savior.

Yet, at times, yea, at diverse times I feel as a man in a desert; as a man lost and undone.

I cannot seem to reach thee, my Lord. I cannot seem to make my voice heard by my God.

I will trust in God with all my heart. I will hold fast to the promises of the Most High, for I know thou hast said that thou wilt never leave me nor forsake me. Thou hast promised me thy comfort and thy love, for neither life nor death nor principalities nor powers, nor things in heaven or on earth can separate me from the love of my God that is in Christ Jesus.

Though I may feel that I am not being heard, that my voice flies off on the wind and is not heard, yet I know that the ear of my God is tuned to me; that the Lord my Savior is my constant companion and that he hears me when I call.

Though I may feel alone and desolate, behold, my God is with me.

I may not feel like dancing but my heart is steadfast in my God.

I may not feel like singing, yet, I will trust the Lord.

Thy Spirit is within me and thy power is tabernacled within thy servant and this I know right well.

My soul may be heavy within me, yet I open my mouth and my spirit binds with the Spirit of the Most High, Jesus my Lord and my voice comes forth in the voice of the Spirit.

I know that my Redeemer lives and that I shall stand in His Presence at the sound of the last trumpet, and I will live forever in His Presence for His love for me is everlasting and His Spirit has sealed me into His family.

Though I may not feel like shouting, yet I will praise the Lord my God.

Though I may not feel like I have the voice to sing, yet will I rejoice in Jesus Christ my God and King.

I may feel like the heavens are brass, and I may feel like a man in a desert, but I know my praises come before my God and I know His ear hears my worship and intunes to my adoration.

Nothing shall keep me from declaring the glory of the Lord my God.

Nothing shall prevent my voice from praising my Lord Christ. For He is my God and His life hath given me life and life more abundantly. Praise be to His mighty name.

Psalm 50

Give me the heart of thy servant David, O Lord: Give me a spirit of praise.

Let me disregard those that surround me and let me see only Jesus my God.

Even as David didst dance before the Ark of the Covenant when it didst return to Jerusalem so let me dance with abandon at the mention of the Lord my God.

Give me the voice of thy servant David, O Lord; let me break forth in singing.

Let all that is within me praise the name of the Lord.

Give me a voice of praise, a heart of adoration, and a spirit of worship, O God.

Let me forever stand in adoration of the Lord.

Give me the resolve of Jeremiah, O Lord, and let thy Word be as a fire shut up within my bones that I might not contain it but must break forth with a testimony to the One true God.

Let me not hear the cries of those that fling despite in my face and let me continue to only speak the Truth of the power of the name of Jesus.

Even as Jeremiah didst continue to speak the Word of the Lord, though the people didst not heed his voice, so let me be with thy Gospel, Lord Jesus. Let nothing restrain me from proclaiming the workings of the Lord, who didst die and resurrect and liveth forevermore.

Give me the determination of Jeremiah, O Lord: let me continually speak forth thy power and majesty.

Let all that is within me praise the name of the Lord.

Give me the spirit of Elisha, O Lord, who didst ask for a double portion of the anointing that didst rest on Elijah.

Let me desire only to walk in thy power and show forth thy strength to the world.

Even as the mantle didst fall upon Elisha so let thine anointing cover me.

Give me a desire to show thy glory by thy power. Let the Spirit of the Lord consume me. Let the Spirit of God clothe me and let thy power indwell me O thou Ancient of Days.

Lord Jesus, my God, my sovereign and King, let me with steadfast determination deliver thy Word to the congregations of the earth. With the strength of thy might let me show forth thy power. Spirit of God use me as thy vessel and let me forever proclaim that Jesus Christ is Lord.

Let all that is within me praise the name of the Lord.

Psalm 51

O Lord, my Lord, how excellent is thy name in all the earth. The mountains tremble at thy footstep and the hills quake at the sound of thy voice.

The Lord is a great and mighty God; He hath no part of sinners, yea the ungodly shall perish as dry grass.

The Word of the Lord is a sweet melody; a song in the night that satisfies the soul.

The wicked know not this sweetness; the unrighteous turn to bitterness all that is within them.

The people of God stand in white raiment; they have washed their robes in the Blood of the Lamb and have made them clean.

The wicked seek for peace yet their lives are filled with turmoil; they seek for solace but find only unrest.

The Lord is a refuge to the needy; to those that acknowledge their need is the Lord as a strong arm of support.

Nothing shall stand in the way of the Blood-bought; those that call upon the Lord in faith will shine like the sun and blind the ungodly with His radiance.

Disorder and chaos is the lot of the wicked; their ways lead only to destruction.

Mayhem and confusion consume those that reject God; their eyes see not His mercy nor His love which He hath lavished on mankind by the death and resurrection of the Christ.

Instability shall be the habitation of the wicked; but the righteous know the power of the Lord in His Presence.

The ungodly seek for peace; they try to find a safe refuge.

But the people of the Lord know rest in His Spirit: the Holy One doth dwell in them and they are secure in Him.

The people of the Lord are safe upon the highway of holiness: the Spirit doth lead, guide, and teach those that call upon His name in faith and in Him they find His righteousness and are blessed.

Praise is the reverberating shouts of the righteous; the wicked know only sorrow in their rejection of the Lord

The people of God sings praises to the Lord Jesus and rejoice in His salvation: but the wicked are heading towards destruction and care not.

O Lord, our Lord, how excellent is thy name in all the earth; thy Church is filled with thy glory.

Psalm 52

The Word of the Lord is a quick and powerful sword: the righteous are defended by its power.

The voice of the Lord speaks in power; the heathen hear his voice and quake.

The children of the Lord seek only the will of the Lord: joy belongs to those that trust in their God.

The Spirit of the Lord tabernacles within those that are washed in the Blood of Jesus: those that surrender to the infilling of the Spirit live in sanctified power.

Let praise arise in the Blood-bought: let the voices of the children of the Most High shout with joy for His salvation.

The Lord reigns; let the earth rejoice.

Praise ye the Lord all ye rocks and valleys, mountains and hills, forest and glades give Him praise.

For the Lord is God over all the earth; the righteous seek him with all their hearts but the wicked disregard His creation.

Pour forth in praise all you who know Jesus the Lord; sing and dance ye who have been washed and whose robes are spotless.

The people of God rejoice in His Word: it is a light to their pathways and a guide in dark times.

Honor His name all you who call upon Jesus for His name is above every name and at the name of Jesus every knee shall bow and every tongue confess that Jesus Christ is Lord to the glory of God the Father.

Let the people arise and bless the name of the Lord; let all who walk in sanctification praise His holy Name.

Glory and honor, dominion and power are His forever and ever: For the Lord had no beginning and He will have no end: Of His kingdom and His majesty there shall be no termination for the Lord lives. Blessed be His name.

Psalm 53

The people of God are a church of the Spirit: this is the love of God in Christ Jesus.

The Spirit brings forth fruit from those of faith: this is the love of God in Christ Jesus.

Love flows freely like a river of living water: this is the love of God in Christ Jesus.

Joy springs forth even in times of trouble: this is the love of God in Christ Jesus.

Peace abides in the hearts of the faithful: this is the love of God in Christ Jesus.

Long-suffering is the hallmark of the redeemed: this is the love of God in Christ Jesus.

Gentleness shines in the lives of the Blood-bought: this is the love of God in Christ Jesus.

The Spirit inspires goodness in all who submit to His will: this is the love of God in Christ Jesus.

Faith is a shield wielded along with the sword of the Spirit which is the Word of God: this is the love of God in Christ Jesus.

Repentance brings redemption when calling on the name of the Lord and those that repent are fruitful ground for the working of the Spirit of God: this is the love of God in Christ Jesus.

The word of wisdom is revealed by the Spirit: this is the love of God in Christ Jesus.

The word of knowledge breaks forth from the same Spirit: this is the love of God in Christ Jesus.

Faith is born and grows and is empowered by the Holy Ghost: this is the love of God in Christ Jesus.

Healing was bought by the stripes of the Savior and works through His servants by His Spirit: this is the love of God in Christ Jesus.

The Spirit bring forth the working of miracles in the faithful: this is the love of God in Christ Jesus.

Prophecy by the Spirit shines in radiance in those that He doth choose: this is the love of God in Christ Jesus.

By the power of the Spirit are diverse kinds of tongues: this is the love of God in Christ Jesus.

By the same Spirit is the interpretation of tongues: this is the love of God in Christ Jesus.

For the Master didst say that He would not leave us comfortless but that He would come to us: His Spirit, the Holy Ghost fills, sustains and guides the faithful: this is the love of God in Christ Jesus.

Psalm 54

Hear, O Church, the Lord our God is One; and thou shalt love the Lord thy God with all thy heart, with all thy soul, with all thy mind and all thy strength.

Hear, O Church, the Lord our God is One; and thou shalt obey the Word of the Lord and proclaim His salvation throughout the earth.

Hear, O Church, the Lord our God is One: and thou shalt bow before His Throne and proclaim that Jesus Christ is Lord to the glory of God the Father.

Hear, O Church, the Lord our God is One: and thou shalt be washed in the Blood of the Lamb and filled with His Spirit that thou mayest be a servant of the Most High.

Hear, O Church, the Lord our God is One: and thou shalt live in holiness even as the Lord thy God is Holy.

Hear, O Church, the Lord our God is One: and thou shalt bless the Lord at all time. His praise shall continually be in thy mouth.

Hear, O Church, the Lord our God is One: and thou shalt glorify God in all that thou art and all that thou doest. Thy life shall be as His will desires.

Hear, O Church, the Lord our God is One: and by His power thou shalt bring His wonders to the earth showing forth His might by the power and glory of His Spirit within thee.

Hear, O Church, the Lord thy God is One: and thou shalt proclaim the Lordship of Jesus the Christ to all the earth; for He hath redeemed thee and hath bought thee with a price.

Hear, O Church, the Lord our God is One: and unto all the earth thou shalt preach the Gospel to every creature.

Hear, O Church, the Lord our God is One: and thou shalt proclaim there is One Lord, one faith and one baptism, giving praise to the name of Jesus for His power.

Hear, O Church, the Lord our God is One: and thou shalt watch and be ready for thou knowest not the time of thy Lord's return. He shall break forth from heaven and call forth all the saints living and sleeping to meet the Lord in the air.

Hear, O Church, the Lord our God is One: and thou shalt love the Lord thy God with all thy heart, with all thy soul, with all thy mind, and with all thy strength.

Hear, O Church, the Lord our God is One: and thou shalt love thy neighbor as thyself, giving honor to the lowly and being a servant unto all thy brethren.

Psalm 55

Let the people of God arise and give honor to the Lord their God; blessed be the name of Jesus.

The Lord watches over those that are His children: He cares for his people as a shepherd.

Give ear to thine elders ye young ones: for the Lord gives wisdom with age and the gray head is a sign of honor from the Lord.

Rise up ye people and bless the Lord: His name is exalted in all the heavens and the earth.

The Lord hath spoken and His word shall not return void: The Word of the Lord shall not pass away.

The wicked see not their sins, nor do they give heed to iniquity: but the people of God repent and bow their hearts to the Throne of the Living God.

Those that know not God are as a desert: their lives are dry and void.

The people of God are as the cedars of Lebanon: they stand strong and firm and grow in strength.

Rejoice ye daughters of the righteous: sing ye sons of the redeemed.

Dance and be glad all ye who love the Lord: for thy God taketh pleasure in thy praise.

Give unto the Lord honor and glory: for Jesus hath brought salvation to those of faith in Him.

Let the name of Jesus be proclaimed throughout the earth: for His love hath been shed abroad in our hearts by the Holy Ghost.

Calvary doth stand as a monument: as a memorial of His love doth it continue.

Bring to the Lord your praises, O ye people of the Blood: you who have washed your garments in the Blood of the Lamb and hath, by faith, given thy lives to the Lord Jesus the Christ.

Bring forth thine offerings and thy gifts to the house of the Lord: for He hath opened the windows of heaven and hath pour out blessings upon thee.

Thou art blessed of God for His love surrounds thee and sustains thee.

Praise the Lord ye people of the Lord: give glory to His holy name.

Psalm 56

The mountain of the Lord doth stand in Zion: the temple of the Lord stood upon it.

The House of the Almighty One was His habitation and His glory didst shine in the Holy of Holies.

While the temple didst stand the veil closed off His Presence lest His glory be revealed and the unrighteous be smitten.

Behold the altar of sacrifice is gone: the laver is done away with.

The Holy Place no longer houses the golden candlestick: there is no bread upon the table of shewbread, neither is there incense on the altar.

The veil hath been torn; yea sundered from top to bottom.

God is no longer housed in a temple made by hands: His habitation is the hearts of those who come to Him in repentance and faith: He is their Lord and they are His people.

There is no longer a veil, for the glory of the Lord hath been revealed in the person of the Christ: Jesus hath shown forth the majesty of God in human flesh.

Let all the earth rejoice for though the temple stands no more yet hath God chosen to make the hearts of men His temple by the Holy Ghost.

The cloud did fill the temple but now doth the Spirit cover the souls of those that believe.

Christ doth reign; yea, the God of the ages is revealed and we have beheld His glory: the glory of the only begotten of the Father, full of grace and truth.

Repent and be baptized therefore that thou mayest receive the Holy Ghost: for the promise is to you and to your children and to those that are afar off, even as many as the Lord our God shall call.

The mountain of the Lord doth stand in Zion: the temple of the Lord is in the hearts of men.

Psalm 57

I will love thee, O Lord, my strength.

The Lord is my rock, and my fortress, and my deliverer; my God, my strength in whom I will trust; my armor, my shield of salvation, and my high tower.

The Lord is the light of my life; my pathway is brightened by His glory and His Word shines upon my path.

In times of distress I called upon the Lord and He heard me out of His holy Heaven; my words came even unto His ears.

The Lord upholds His children; as a hen covers her chicks doth the Spirit of the Lord hover over those that are His.

I will bless thee, O Lord, by my life; I will give all that I am unto the Lord that I may be His possession.

Therefore hath the Lord recompensed me according to my righteousness, according to the cleanness of my heart.

The Lord liveth and blessed be my Rock: and let the God of my salvation be exalted.

Therefore I will give thanks unto thee, O Lord, among the brethren, and I will sing praises unto thy name.

How blessed are the people of the Lord: for His Spirit doth make them His habitation and they are clothed with the white robes of the righteousness of the Holy Ghost.

I will give praise to the Lord Jesus, for His mercy and grace doth cover me as a garment; yea, as a cloak am I compassed about by His love.

The seraphim give praises of His holiness continually around the Throne; the praises of the Lord Jesus resounds throughout the throne room.

Behold, how strong a Rock is the Lord Jesus Christ; He is a sure and certain foundation, and my life is build upon Him for He is my God.

From the rising of the sun to the going down of the same, the name of the Lord Jesus is to be praised.

Throughout all the earth, even the cries of angels flying on the winds, shall praise the name of our God.

Psalm 58

Lift up your heads, O ye gates; and be ye lift up ye everlastings doors; and the King of Glory shall come in.

Who is the King of Glory? The Lord strong and mighty, the Lord mighty in battle.

Lift up your heads, O ye gates; and be ye lift up ye everlasting doors; and the King of Glory shall come in.

Who is the King of Glory? The Lord of Hosts, Jesus, Lord of all, He is the King of Glory.

They didst crucify the Lord of Glory; they reviled His name and did Him despite.

The rulers turned their backs upon Him; their cry was to crucify Him.

He wast nailed to the cross and the iniquities of us all were upon Him; He did suffer the pains of sin upon His holy and sinless person, and He felt the Father turning from the sin that was upon Him.

Lift up your heads, O ye gates; and be ye lift up ye everlasting doors; and the King of Glory shall come in.

Who is the King of Glory? The Risen One, the Conqueror of death, hell and the grave, He is the King of Glory.

Give praise to the One who took our sins, was crucified, dead, buried, and rose again.

Give glory to the Lord Jesus for His love hath bought us salvation; His grace took the payment for our sins.

How amazing is the grace of the Lord our God? How broad is the scope of His mercy for those that love Him?

Though thou werest cut from the land of the living, yet didst thou rise from the dead in victory and power.

Glory to the Risen Lord; Who is the King of Glory; the Lord strong and mighty; the Lord mighty to save, Jesus, He is the King of Glory!

Psalm 59

Why art thou weary and downcast, O my soul? The Lord thy God is thy sustenance.

Why dost thou sigh and let thy spirit groan within thee? Jesus hath taken thy burdens.

This world is not my home; I am an alien and a foreigner in a foreign land.

I belong not in this place. This world is not my home.

My spirit sighs; I long for that which is ahead of me, my eternal Home.

My heart longs to cry, Maranatha, O Lord; come Jesus and take thy people.

Yet I am restrained from this cry, for many yet need to hear; the Gospel yet needs to be preached to those that have not yet heard.

Though I feel as a foreigner, yet I must endure and tarry for my Home is yet ahead; my Home awaits for the Lord hath made for me a mansion.

My soul longs for the Presence of the One who hath shed His grace on me; the Lord Jesus who hath given me His love and hath shown me mercy.

How dost thou try and contain me, O earth? I am a foreigner in this world.

How dost thou try and hold me, O world? Heaven awaits me and, behold, the Lord Jesus holds out His hands to welcome me Home.

This world is not my Home, behold, I am passing through as a wanderer; as a nomad am I in this place.

Cry out, O my soul, for all that thou dost know is that I am not Home yet; this is not where I belong.

Though I am weary of waiting and my soul at times seems to faint within me for longing, yet the Gospel must go forth; new souls must be added to the Kingdom of my Lord Christ.

Hold off thy return, thou Lord of my life; let not the trumpet sound announcing thy return. For many there be that need thee; yea, many yet need to hear of thee.

Stand firm, O soul within me; hold fast to the strength of the power of the Spirit of thy God.

Thy Home is set, O my soul, thou needest not to grieve. Thy God alone knowest the time of the return of the Lord Christ.

Hold fast within me, O my soul; proclaim salvation until the trumpet doth sound.

Be strong in the Lord and in the power of His mighty; rest in the strength of His Spirit that doth dwell within thee and spread forth the Gospel until thou art called Home.

Psalm 60

Thou hast kept me in peace, O Lord my God; thou art my sure and certain hope.

Thy grace doth cover me as a garment; yea, as a cloak of fine weaving art thou my covering.

Though I was dead in my trespasses and sins still thou didst love me and send the Lord Christ to die for me.

Thou hast upheld me by thy mercy and sustained me by thy Grace. For thou art a great and awesome God and there is none like thee. Thou, and thou alone, art God.

The Lord is my Rock and my salvation; as water didst flow from the rock in the desert as the people of Israel didst journey, so thy Word doth declare that Rock was Christ: you are water in a desert and thou dost quench the thirsting of my soul.

Behold, how gracious is the Lord God of Hosts: How merciful is the Lord.

He hath shed His love abroad in our hearts by the Holy Ghost and His power doth dwell in the hearts of those that have trusted Him by faith.

Great is the Lord and greatly to be praised; let the high praises of the Lord be shouted by the Blood-bought. Let the voices of the redeemed ring out the joyous songs of His amazing grace.

How beautiful is the name of Jesus; How glorious is His workings of salvation for His people.

He is exalted above the heavens: His name is above every name.

There is no one like our God, yea there is none like the Lord Jesus Christ.

He is the perfect Lamb sacrificed for the sins of the world. There was no spot of blemish in Him: no sin was on Him and He committed no iniquity.

Yet the chastisement of our peace was upon Him and by His stripes we are healed.

He was despised and rejected of men: a man of sorrows and acquainted with grief; yet we esteemed Him not, neither didst we recognize Him as God while in the flesh.

But, praise be to God, though He was crucified, dead and buried, yet He didst rise to life everlasting and glorious that we too may become the sons of God.

Praised be the name of the Risen One: glory and honor to the Lord Jesus: for He alone is God: He alone is Lord of all.

Glory to the name of the Lord. Hallelujah!

Psalm 61

Sing unto the Lord a new song: sing forth the choruses of praise to the Lord thy God.

Sing and be joyous, ye people of the Name for He hath done marvelous things.

Sing to the Lord, the songs of Home; when the roll is called up yonder: I'll fly away: It will be worth it all.

Joyously proclaim the praises of our God: His Name is wonderful: My Jesus I love Thee: Glory to His Name.

O for a thousand tongues to sing my great Redeemer's praise: the glories of my God and King the triumphs of His grace.

Break forth in singing ye who know the Lord: let the music of the Kingdom of our God rise forth and be glad: He hath made me glad: He brought me out of the miry clay: Glory, glory, glory, somebody touched me.

For the hand of the Lord hath been favorable to His people: He hath given them grace and hath justified them by His Blood.

Let the people of God rejoice: Let those who have tasted His salvation through His Blood be thankful and give Him praise:

Praise Him! Praise Him, Jesus our blessed Redeemer. Sing, O earth, His wonderful love proclaim. Hail Him! Hail Him, Highest archangel in glory. Strength and honor give to His holy name.

The name of Jesus is so sweet. I love its music to repeat.

It's shouting time in heaven. A sinner once lost is found.

Sing unto God the songs of redemption: Redeemed how I love to proclaim it. Redeemed by the Blood of the Lamb: redeemed by His excellent mercies: His child and forever I am.

Praise the name of Jesus. He's my Rock. He's my fortress. He's my Deliverer in Him will I trust. Praise the name of Jesus!

When we stand in thy Presence, O God, thy people shall, for eternity, sing praises and honor to thy name. Ten thousand years and we will just be started: ten thousand years, we will just have begun.

When we've been there ten thousand years, bright shining as the sun, we've no less days to sing God's praise then when we first begun.

Praise ye the Lord, O His people. Sing and be glad for thy God hath broken the chains of sin and hath redeemed thee to everlasting life through Jesus Christ our Lord.

Sing unto the Lord a new song: let His praise be glorious.

Psalm 62

I will glorify the Lord my God and give praises unto the King of Heaven.

He who sits upon the Throne of Grace is worthy of all praise.

I will stand in the congregation of the Blood-bought and give testimony to the marvelous grace of our loving Lord.

In the sanctuary of my God will I give praise and honor to His holy name.

The Lord Jesus Christ is highly to be praised; His glory covers the earth and His power is displayed through His saints.

I will magnify the Lord at all times: His praise shall continually be in my mouth.

The Lord of Hosts is a mighty God: full of compassion and abounding in grace towards those that call upon His name.

I will come into the Presence of the Lord with gladness and with my voice will I give praises to His name.

The name of the Lord Jesus is the name above all names: His power is without limit and His glory is unsearchable.

I will say of the Lord, He is my God and testify of His loving grace throughout all the earth.

The Lord stands knocking at the door: if anyone will open the door, He will come in to them and be with them.

I will shout praises to the Lord in the sanctuary: in the house of my God will I give Him glory.

The Lord is seeking those that are to be saved: His hands are open to all who come to Him in faith.

I will testify of the power of my God: the strength of His Spirit's power is limitless.

The Lord hath said, come unto me all that are weary and heavy laden and I will give thee rest.

I will say of the Lord, His power is matchless and His glory surrounds His people: those that are called by the name of the Lord will give praises unto His name.

The Lord hath said, Lo, I come quickly: the return of the Lord Jesus is imminent.

I will look to the skies and wait: I will teary until He comes. Until the Day of the Lord will I give praises unto the name of the Lord my God: to the name of Jesus will I ascribe praise.

Psalm 63

Let the glory of the Lord arise: make His praise glorious.

The Lord of Grace is a mighty and powerful God full of wonders and lovingly compassionate.

Rise up, O earth, and extol the name of the Most High: give glory to the name of Jesus for He is a wondrous God.

Let the people of the Lord dance in His Presence: let those who are called by the name of the Lord dance for joy and be glad.

For the Lord is God over all the earth: His power is displayed in all His creation.

Shout unto God all ye people: praise the name of the Glorious One.

Honor and glory, dominion and power are ascribed unto the Lord God of Hosts.

Let the praises of the Captain of the Armies of the Lord resound throughout the heavens.

Come ye people of God and worship His name: bless the Lord and give honor unto His majesty.

Praise the Lord: Glorify His name: give unto the Lord the honor due to His name.

For the name of our God is a name above all names: the name of Jesus is full of power: let all the earth tremble before His glory.

Let the Church arise: let the Blood-bought rejoice and be glad in the name of Jesus.

Lord Christ thy name is glorious: thy people bow before thee and are glad.

Psalm 64

Mine enemies doth surround me: break forth, O God, and defend me.

I am encompassed about by those that hate me: the Lord of Hosts is my refuge.

Let mine enemies be desolate for the Lord is against them: the enemies of my soul shall be brought down to the pit: they shall dwell eternally in the fiery depths.

Only those that are righteous, whom the Lord God hath chosen shall inherit eternal life through Jesus Christ the Lord.

Those that come against me are proud in their own deceit: the Lord shall destroy the workings of the enemy.

They call one to another and give voice to their treachery: the Lord shall consume them in fire: they shall be utterly undone.

Trickery, sham, duplicity, and guile are the workings of the enemies of the Lord's hosts: the righteous shall rise up against them and the hosts of Heaven shall defeat them.

There is no honesty in those that know not God: lies and the father of lies is the enemy of souls.

The righteous are not so: they shall rise on eagle's wings and ride upon the storms for the Lord Jesus is their strength and His Spirit is their empowerment.

The people of the Lord rejoice only in the strength of their God for they know that 'tis not by might nor by power but by my Spirit, sayeth the Lord.

All have sinned and come short of the glory of God: but Christ hath given His life that sin might be abolished.

Yea, the Lord hath said, if we confess our sins He is faithful and just to forgive us our sins and to cleanse us from all unrighteousness: this hath been the purchase of the cross: the life of Jesus hath given us the victory.

The people of the Lord: the Blood-bought: the redeemed know that the Spirit is their strength: The Holy Ghost hath made the people of the Lord His habitation.

They are empowered by the Spirit of the Lord: those that have been washed in the Blood of Jesus rejoice in the might of their God.

Though the enemy may rise up and though those that are against me may arise to do me harm, yet the Spirit of the Lord doth raise up a standard against them and the Blood-stained banner of the redeemed shall be their identity in Christ Jesus the Lord.

Psalm 65

My soul doth long for my God: yea for the courts of my God do I yearn.

Set me before thy Throne, O God that I may bring to thee the sacrifice of praise.

Within the heavenly tabernacle do I long to abide: the courts of the Lord shall be my rest.

Bring me into thy Presence, O God: cover me with thy Spirit and let me be clothed by thy radiance.

Into the Kingdom of my God shall I fly: my soul shall ever be with the Lord.

Though I be absent in body yet in the Presence of my Lord Jesus shall I stand: I know that my Redeemer liveth and that at the last trump I shall be called into His glory.

Thou hast promised that thou hast builded a mansion for thy saints: but, lo, I need not a mansion, just a place at the Throne.

In the Presence of God shall I dance and rejoice: in the glory of the Most High shall His saints praise His name.

The Lord liveth: Let the saints proclaim His glory. The Lord is an everlasting God. Let the children of the Lord praise His name.

Around the throne of the Lord doth the Seraphim fly: they do cry one to another, holy, holy, holy, is the Lord God Almighty.

The children of the Lord shall stand in His Presence and proclaim with a loud voice the mercy and grace of the Lord Jesus Christ.

Thy glory shall be the light of thy people: there in His Presence shall be no need of sun or moon for the Lamb is the light.

The people of the Lord shall dwell in His palace: in the Kingdom of our God shall the righteous be blessed.

My soul, O God, doth long for thee: behold I am not Home yet, yea this is not where thy people belong: take all of this world,

O Lord, but give me Jesus: in the Presence of my God doth my soul long to be.

Sound the ram's horn trumpet, ye Archangel that the dead in Christ may rise first, then those that are alive and remain may be caught up together with them in the clouds to meet the Lord in the air: thus shall we ever be with the Lord.

Psalm 66

Thy throne, O God, is in heaven: thou sittest upon the winds and thou doest ride the whirlwind like a chariot.

Let the people of God arise and cast off their sinful ways that they may be holiness unto the Lord.

Cry to the Lord and seek His mercy, ye children of men: seek ye first the kingdom of God and His righteousness that thou mayest be holiness unto the Lord.

Break off the shackles of iniquity from us, O God, that we may holiness unto the Lord.

Let grace arise and mercy be shown to those that repent before thee, O God, that we may be holiness unto the Lord.

Thou hast said, O Lord, that obedience is better than sacrifice: thou seekest a pure heart.

Cast off thy frailty ye children of men: take up the power of the Spirit of the Lord that He may strengthen thee and sustain thee.

Wash ye in the blood of Jesus: let all the stains of sins be purified by the cleansing flow of Calvary: be thou holiness unto the Lord.

Take upon thee the white robes of the righteousness of the Lord that thou mayest be holiness unto the Lord.

Thou hast spoken, O God, and thou canst not lie: thou hast said, without holiness no man shall see God: let all the people of Jesus' name be holiness unto the Lord.

Arise men of faith: wake ye daughters of the Name: stand before thy God in holiness.

Let iniquity be washed in the Blood: let all trespasses and sins be cleansed by the shed Blood of Jesus: let all who walk in the Spirit be holiness unto the Lord.

Submit to the Spirit: let a new heart of flesh be given thee by the Holy One.

The Lord doth desire to conform thee, ye who come to His Presence by faith: yea, he doth long to make thee into the image of the Lord Jesus that thou mayest be holiness unto the Lord.

Ye who follow the Nazarene, be thou, in sincerity of heart, mind, soul, and body, holiness unto the Lord.

The Lord reigneth in heaven: the hearts of men are His dwelling place by faith: be ye therefore, holiness unto the Lord.

Psalm 67

Give me faith, O Lord, to trust in thee: give me a heart that fully trusteth in thee, O Lord.

Thy Word is truth: thou art the Way the Truth and the Life: thou, O Lord Jesus, art Truth incarnate.

Lord, I believe: help thou my unbelief.

My confidence is in thee, O Lord: break thou my unbelief and raise me in full faith in thee alone.

Thy Word is sure: thou art an unchanging God: thou art the same yesterday, today, and forever.

Give me, O God, a heart of faith: take all from me that is unbelieving and replace it with faith in thee alone.

Raise me as a man of faith: let my confidence be in thee alone, O Lord my God.

Thou art my strength; in thee do I trust. Thou art the Rock of my foundation: in thee and thy Word do I put my devotion.

O Lord, my Lord, how can I even conceive of not putting my full reliance in thee alone? Thou art my God and thou canst not lie. Thou hast promised: help me to rely solely on thy promises O God and trust in thy Word that my faith may rise to thee and see the wonders that thou hast for me.

Thou art God: Thou canst do anything; yea, nothing is impossible with thee: truly nothing is impossible to him that believeth.

Lord, I believe: help thou my unbelief.

Thou knowest, Lord Jesus, my heart: thou knowest that I trust in thee. Eradicate all that is within me that is not of faith in thee alone: Cut off from me all that is not solely concentrated on thee, O Lord.

My heart fails me: my faith is weak and my confidence is feeble.

Let not my feeble confidence rule within me, O Lord my God: take out this scrawny faith and replace it with full certainty, conviction, and assurance in thee alone.

Help me, O Lord, to fully trust in thy Word that what thou hast said is to me already done and complete even before I ask.

Make me a man of faith, O Lord: consume me by thy Spirit, O My God, and place within me a heart fully confident in thee and thy Word alone.

Be gone from me all spirits of unbelief: be thou removed and cast into the sea that the Lord only shall be my support and thy Word my sure and ultimate confidence.

Rise and be healed, O my soul: let faith arise in thy heart. Rise and be healed in the name of Jesus. Come thou Spirit of Christ and take over all that mayest be in me that is not of faith and replace it with thy strength. Work in me only faith, O God.

Psalm 68

I need thee, O Lord: I need thee. I need thy strength and thy power: I need thy mind to be builded within me.

My soul is weak, yea, my strength is undone, and I am weak and feeble.

Be thou my strength, O Lord, that in the name of Jesus nothing shall be impossible.

Be thou my sure confidence that thy Word may arise in faith within me and thy power mayest be displayed in me.

Thou art a God of great power: yea, thou art a God of the impossible: what seemeth impossible to man is but as nothing to thee. Thou canst do anything: there is nothing unworkable with thee, O Lord Jesus, my God and my sure confidence.

Thou didst speak the universe into being and nothing is outside of thy ability.

Create in me a heart of faith, Lord Jesus: make of me a man after thine own heart.

Thou art my desire, O God: the world and all it contains is as dung to me.

Strengthen me, O God, by thy power: mold me into thine own image, O Lord.

Thou art to me my all in all: the heathen know not thy power, nor thy glory.

Shower me, Holy Spirit, with thy might: let thy power pour forth on me.

Change me. Mold me. Be thou as a potter and form in me thy glorious power.

Arise within me in might, O thou that hast formed the worlds: thou who hast spoken and the universe came into being.

Speak again, O God, and let thy voice speak thy power into thy servant.

I will praise thee, O Lord, with my whole heart: with all my being will I give glory to the name of Jesus, my God.

Psalm 69

Grant me a vision, O God, of what couldst be by thy power.

Grant me, O Lord, an insight into what is possible with thee.

Take from me, Jehovah-Rapha, my Healer, my spirit of timidity and grant me a vision of thy great power.

My soul doth praise thee, O God, and thou knowest my heart: yea thou didst know me whilest I was still within my mother's womb. Thou knowest my uprising and mine outgoing.

Thou knowest me, O God: thou doest know my heart and my desires.

Let me see through thine eyes, O God: Lord Jesus, grant me thy vision that I may know and witness thy glorious power in all its fullness.

Make me thy hands and feet to the people, O Lord: make me thy true servant that thy glory mayest be seen through thy bondsman.

Thou changest not. Thy Word is not altered nor doth it change.

Thou art a God of verity: yea, thou thyself art Truth, there is no falseness in thee.

If thy Word doth say it, let me, Lord, grasp hold of thy power to see it done in Jesus' name.

Pour into me the kind of faith that sees all thy power displayed: nothing is impossible with thee, O Lord God of Hosts.

Make me an instrument of thy glory, Lord Jesus: use me as thou wouldst that thou mayest be glorified.

Make me humble before thee, O Lord: let not my soul be exalted within myself.

Rise up in me, O God: rise up and show thyself glorious through thy servant.

Thy name shall be praised in all the earth, O God: thou art a God worthy of all praise.

Show thyself glorious through thy servant: break out within me in great faith, O Lord.

Let mine enemies be put to shame for thou art a God of power and might.

May those that know thee be drawn to thee and let thy power draw them as a moth to a flame.

Rise up in me O Power of God, Holy Spirit of Might: demonstrate thy glory that those that know thee not may see thy strength and come to know thee in truth.

O my God, I long to be an instrument of thy glory: yea my soul doth long to be used by the hand of my God.

Psalm 70

The power of the Lord is above all that are called gods: great is the love of God.

The might of the Lord is greater than ten thousand times ten thousand: great is the love of God.

The glory of the Lord is displayed in His handiwork: great is the love of God.

The universe and all that is in it is the working of His voice: great is the love of God.

The Lord rideth on the winds, His footsteps make the earth to tremble: great is the love of God.

The strength of the Lord is greater than that of horses: great is the love of God.

Greater than the vigor of many men is the might of the Lord; great is the love of God.

The Lord saw the sins of man and took upon Himself the form of a servant: great is the love of God.

In the form of a servant did He become obedient unto death: great is the love of God.

Obedient unto death, even the death of the cross: great is the love of God.

Death could not hold Him, neither could the grave restrain Him: great is the love of God.

Risen from the dead and risen in great power is the Lord Christ: great is the love of God.

Ascended on high and seated at the right hand of the Father: great is the love of God.

The Lord loveth all that call upon the name of Jesus: great is the love of God.

The power of His Spirit is available to all that trust in His name: great is the love of God.

Baptism and filling in the power of the Spirit is the promise of the Father: great is the love of God.

The might of the Lord is within His Spirit: great is the love of God.

The Spirit of the Lord giveth to all according to His will: great is the love of God.

The Lord Jesus is Lord over all the heavens and the earth: great is the love of God.

No man cometh unto the Father but by Him: great is the love of God.

Neither is there salvation in any other name: great is the love of God.

The Lord grants grace to all according to His mercy: great is the love of God.

The grace of the Lord is abundant and free: great is the love of God.

Power and glory, majesty and dominion are in the name of Jesus: great is the love of God.

There is no lack of strength in the name of the Lord: great is the love of God.

His stretched forth His word and the worlds were formed: great is the love of God.

His hands formed man from the dust of the earth: great is the love of God.

He breathed into man the breath of lives and man became a living soul: great is the love of God.

The Lord has mercy to all that come to Him by faith: great is the love of God.

All that come to His Throne by faith are clothed in the robes of His righteousness: great is the love of God.

In the white robes of His righteousness doth He clothe His saints: great is the love of God.

Into the realms of Glory shall He call His people: great is the love of God.

At the sound of the trumpet and the voice of the Archangel shall His people be called: great is the love of God.

By His Spirit shall He quicken those that sleep: great is the love of God.

Those that sleep shall not prevent those that are alive and remain: great is the love of God.

By the power of the Lord shall we all be changed: great is the love of God.

In a moment, in the twinkling of an eye shall we all be changed: great is the love of God.

And so shall we ever be with the Lord: great is the love of God.

Ten thousand times ten thousand years shall we begin to glorify the name of Jesus: great is the love of God.

In His Presence shall His saints forever rejoice: great is the love of God.

No tear shall fall, neither shall there be any weeping or mourning: great is the love of God.

In the Throne room of Heaven shall His saints give Him praise: great is the love of God.

Before the Throne of our God shall the saints cast their crowns: great is the love of God.

Forever and ever shall the Lord Jesus reign: great is the love of God.

Of His Throne and His kingdom shall there be no end: great is the love of God.

Jesus shall reign over all the Heavens and the earth: great is the love of God.

The power of the name of the Lord shall reign in Glory: great is the love of God.

His people rise up and call Him blessed: great is the love of God.

Nothing shall separate us from the love of God that is in Christ Jesus: great is the love of God.

Psalm 71

My faith reaches towards the heavens: into the throne room of the Most High doth my faith rise.

Thou art my God and in thy Word doth I put my trust: thy Word is verity, thou canst not lie.

Yet feel I weak and the heavens are as brass before my prayers.

I know that thou hearest me, O thou who sleepest not: thou whose ear is always listening, thou doest hear.

Thou hast promised that whatsoever was asked in thy name that thou wouldst do it, and this I believe.

How is it then that my cry unto thee seems to return to me unheard when I knoweth that thine ear is listening?

My faith is weak before thee, O Lord my God, my Savior, my Jesus: my faith is frail and seemeth insubstantial.

Thy Word hath promised that nothing is impossible with thee.

Thou hast said that thou art the God that healeth: Jehovah Rapha art thou.

Lord, I believe. Help thou mine unbelief.

Empower my faith by thy Spirit, O God: the fruit of the Spirit is love, joy, peace, long-suffering, gentleness, meekness, temperance, and faith.

Strengthen my faith, Lord Jesus. Bolster thou my faith, O my God.

Help me to bring what my heart and mind doth know into my spirit and give me a strong faith: a faith that bringeth the impossible into the possible by thy Name and by thy Spirit.

Lord, I believe. Help thou mine unbelief.

Psalm 72

The Lord is a great and mighty God: let the people shout His praises.

Let the glory of the Lord be magnified throughout the earth.

The Lord is gracious and full of compassion: come ye lowly and be covered by His grace.

Let the Name of the Lord be praised in heaven and earth: let the Name of Jesus be exalted.

Sing ye angels and shout ye Saints for the Lord is King over all.

Dance ye daughters and rejoice ye sons: let the praises of the Lord be heard in the camps of the righteous: let the high praises of the Lord resound throughout the Church.

Jesus shall reign over all the earth: He shall be King over all the nations.

All the peoples of the earth shall bow before the Lord Christ for He alone is worthy to receive glory and honor: dominion and power are the Lord's.

The Lord is powerful and glorious: strong and mighty is the Lord God of Hosts.

The mountains quake at the footsteps of the Lord: the valleys tremble at the Presence of the Most High.

The trees of the field shall clap their hands and the row shall leap for joy in praise to the Almighty One.

Glorious is the Lord: the Lord Jesus Christ is a magnificent God: awesome in power and tremendous in strength is He.

Pay tribute to His glory ye His Saints: give honor to His Name ye Blood-washed peoples.

The Lord Jesus is high and Holy: great and mighty is His Name and His power is unsearchable.

Sing forth His praises ye who are clothed in His righteousness: shout and be glad: dance and rejoice ye children of God.

His Blood hath bought thee: His life hath paid the price of thy sins.

From the dead didst He arise in glory: in majesty and power didst He come forth from the grave alive and victorious.

Let the earth see the glory of the Risen One: let the nations bow before Him and sing praises to His name: for the Lord Jesus the Christ is God over all: let the high praises of the Lord be seen throughout the earth.

Psalm 73

None are righteous: no not one.

Iniquity reigns in the hearts of men: condemned by their sins the heathen face eternal damnation.

Sin entered by the arrogance of man looking to become like unto God: sin separated man from the God that had formed him from the dust of the earth.

Woe! unto man who knoweth not the Lord: his ways are headed towards destruction.

Without hope in the Lord devastation is the habitation of the sinful: the hearts of the wicked are filled with conceit: they are without hope in the world.

God hath looked at sinful man and hath had compassion on them: yea, His mercy reaches out to anyone who calls upon Him in faith.

The Lord hath humbled himself and became obedient unto death, even the death of the cross: death could not hold Him: yea, He hath risen to glorious victory for His power is matchless and His love is boundless.

Though man may be lost because of his sins yet hath God, in His loving-kindness, shown unto them His consideration of their lowly estate and hath sent the Lord Jesus to bridge the gap and provide the cleansing of the Blood.

Sin no longer need reign in the hearts of men: for the Lord Christ hath made a way out of the bondage of sin and death and hath conquered and is victorious.

Psalm 74

When I am afraid, the Lord shall be by Guardian.

The Lord my God shall hold me up and encompass me about with His strength.

Nothing shall come against me that the Lord doth not allow: my steps are ordered by the Lord.

Though mine enemies shall rage against me, though I may walk through the camps of the wicked, yet the Lord shall be my protector: His name shall forever be my refuge.

Though I may be weary in spirit, yet doth the power of the Lord come upon me by His glorious Spirit.

Though storms may seethe around me, though a tempest may surround me, yet the Lord is my strong tower: His name shall forever be my fortress.

The wicked know not the comfort of the Lord: their eyes are blind to the goodness of the Lord Christ.

Behold, all ye saints, the Lord Jesus is a strong and mighty God: His arm is not shortened, neither is His power in any way decreased.

When I am worn down and when my strength seemeth gone, the Lord is my power and my delight: His Word shall be my light and His Spirit shall revive my soul though it may be low even unto death.

The will of the Lord is that I shall prosper and be in health even as my soul prospereth: this is the Word of the Lord my God.

In God will I trust: His Spirit comforteth me in distress: yea, in times of trouble the Lord is a wall against mine enemies.

There is no one like the Lord: none there be that are like the Lord God of Hosts.

Great and mighty is the Lord: great and mighty is His name.

The Lord Jesus hath been given a name that is above every name, that at the name of Jesus every knee shall bow and every tongue confess that Jesus Christ is Lord to the glory of God the Father.

When I am weak, the Lord shall strength me: the name of the Lord shall cover me with His power and in His name all affliction shall cease.

There is no God like the Lord: Jesus shall reign forever: His name shall be praised in heaven and on earth.

When I am distressed, though I may be weak within myself, the Lord Jesus shall send His Spirit to comfort and sustain me by His power and might.

The Lord is great: nothing shall come against me that can stand against the name of the Lord my God: blessed be the name of the Lord.

Psalm 75

O Lord, you are my God: my heart is yours, there is no God but thee.

I am thine, O Lord: thou hast loved me 'ere I knew thee and my love is thine.

Thou hast called me from my sins: thou hast washed me in thy Blood: I am thy servant, O Lord God of Hosts.

The Lord my God, Jesus the Holy One is a great and awesome God: there is none like the Lord.

My soul doth magnify the Lord: to the God of my salvation do I raise my praise.

My heart is thy Throne, O Lord: reign thou in me.

The Lord is a God of faithfulness and grace: blessed be His name forevermore.

The Lord is a God of might and power: let His name be exalted.

I am thy servant, O Lord: I bow before thee and call thee blessed.

I was wretched and undone: my life was stained by sin and overcome by my transgressions: but the Lord had mercy on me and called me into His marvelous light.

Thus will I bless the Lord and give the God of my salvation all my praise.

The adoration of my heart shall be thine, O Lord: unto Jesus, my God do I raise my hallelujahs.

Be thankful, O my soul and bless the Lord for His grace: His mercy is ever towards thee, O my heart.

I worship thee, O Prince of Peace: thou hast captured my soul by thy love.

The Lord is a majestic God: His praise shall continually be in my mouth.

Unto the Lord, the God of my salvation, shall I bring my exaltation.

There is none like the Lord: there is no God like the Christ, the Lord Jesus of Nazareth.

My devotion is thine, O Lord: no praise shall I give but unto the Lord Christ: His and His alone are the glory and honor, dominion, and power now and forever.

Receive the words of thy servant, O my God, and be thou blessed by my life lived by thy power.

Spirit of the Most High, make of me a true servant of the One Who Reigns in Glory.

May the words of my mouth and the meditations of my heart be acceptable in thy sight, O Lord my Rock and my Redeemer.

Blessed be the name of the Lord. Hallelujah! Lord Jesus.

Psalm 76

Lord, thou knowest all my desires and deepest longings. My tears are liquid words and thou canst read them all.

When I lay upon my bed and my soul doth cry out to thee, Thou knowest all that is within me.

Let my tears be praise unto thee, O Lord: let the cry of my heart be a sweet savor unto thee, O thou my Rock and my Salvation.

Even as I drench my pillow in the night, O God, let my weeping be thy praise.

No sadness is within me O God. I rejoice in thee, my Lord, who hast loved me.

My tears are the cry of my heart, Lord Jesus: unto thee doth I bow my heart in adoration.

I love thee, Lord, and I lift my heart before thee: be thou exalted within me, O God.

Let thy Spirit consume me that I may live in thee.

Before I was formed, yea, before I didst take shape thou didst know me: thou dost know my outgoings and mine uprisings.

When I rise may my thoughts turn to thee, O Lord my God.

When I lay me down to rest may my thoughts be only of thee, O my God.

Lord, thou hast given me a new heart: thou hast made me a new creature in Christ Jesus.

Therefore will I praise thee in my waking, in my walking throughout my day and as I lay me down at night: the Lord my God, shall forever be the reason for my praise.

I cannot give unto thee all that thou dost deserve of praise, O Lord: my tongue is weak in its ability to give thee glory.

Let my life shine before thee as mine adoration, O Lord.

Let all that is within me give honor and glory to the Lord my Christ.

When I weep before thee, O Lord, may my tears be liquid words of tribute to thy glory.

Psalm 77

Uphold thou me, O Lord my God: fortify thou me in my pursuit of thy righteousness.

Sanctify me by thy truth, O Lord: thy Word is truth.

Thou, in thine own self, art the fullness of all Truth: yea, thou art the Way and Life.

Spirit of the Holy One, sanctify me: wash me in the Blood of Jesus and make me clean before thee.

Clothe me in the white robes of thy righteousness that I may stand before thee in purity of heart and spirit.

Let thy Word be birthed within me that I may not sin against thee.

Hear the cry of my heart O God and sanctify thou me.

Thou art holy, O Lord, and thou desirest holiness of thy people.

Sustain me by thy Word, O Lord: Thou who art the Word made flesh, tabernacle within me that I may be fully thine.

My soul doth reject mine own iniquity: that which hath displeased thee in me, O Lord, doth I detest and abhor.

Thy holiness is my desire, O God of my salvation: Create in me the image of the Lord Jesus, Holy Spirit, that in holiness I may serve thee.

Try me, O God: search my heart and sanctify it as thy throne.

Rule in me, O Lord, that my heart may be thy judgment seat and that thou mayest see in me no iniquity: be it by thine own power resident in me by thy Spirit: the image of the Lord Jesus.

Behold, I was shapen in iniquity and formed in unrighteousness: but thou hast washed me: thou hast cleansed me by thy Blood: thou hast given me thy Spirit and I am purified.

Fully justified shall I stand in thy Presence, O God: clothed in white robes shall I bow before thy Throne and give thee praise.

Thou foundest me lost in transgression but thou hast cast always all iniquity from me by thy Blood.

In thee, O Lord, shall I forever rejoice: for the Lord my God is faithful and just to forgive my sins: yea, thou doth sustain me by thy Spirit and I am thine.

Psalm 78

Open the eyes of the nations, Spirit of the Most High: let thy glory be seen by those that hath been deceived.

Ears have they but they hear not: eyes have they but they see not: they have been blinded by the evil one.

The Lord hath shown His power in all the earth: His creation shows His manifest power.

For the invisible things of him from the creation of the world are clearly seen, being understood by the things that are made, even his eternal power and Godhead; so that they are without excuse.

Open their eyes that they may see and behold that which thou hast done through Christ Jesus the Lord.

O God, God of power and justice, shine the light of the Gospel to those who have been deluded and misled.

The enemy, the father of lies, hath deceived and swindled those tainted by sin.

Though they be without excuse, have mercy on them, O God, and take from their eyes the cataracts of lies.

Spirit of God, through thine own power, break apart the walls of iniquity: let the light of the glorious Gospel of Christ be seen throughout the earth.

Shine, Jesus, shine: let the whole earth be filled with thy radiance: let the Gospel be seen: let iniquity be broken: let chains be shattered and those in bondage released.

Thou art God and thy power is unsearchable: thy glory is beyond compare and thy strength is not slackened.

Bring to thy brightness those that walk in darkness that they may see and behold the blessing of life through Jesus Christ the Lord.

Psalm 79

Let the song of the redeemed arise: Sing out the amazing grace of Jesus.

Raise your voices ye Blood-bought throngs and sing the songs of salvation.

Wonderful grace of Jesus: thank God for the Blood: when the roll is called up yonder.

Lift up thy voice ye sons of God and rejoice in the grace of the Lord.

Magnify the Lord ye daughters of the Lord and sing of His marvelous grace.

Wonderful grace of our loving Lord; grace that exceeds our sin and our guilt; yonder on Calvary's mount outpoured, there where the Blood of the Lamb was spilt.

Let thy voices rival the angels, ye Saints of the Lord: give voice to His mercy and grace.

Seraphim cry the holiness of God: let the redeemed sing the songs of redemption.

Lift up the tymbral and harp: strike the cymbals and sounds forth the trumpets: sing the song of the Blood.

Hear, ye heavens, the chorus of redemption: for chains have been broken: sin has been removed.

Let the song of the redeemed arise: let the Blood-washed sing praises to the name of the Risen One, Jesus the Christ by whose grace ye have been saved.

When I survey the wondrous cross on which the Prince of Glory died, my richest gain I count but loss, and pour contempt on all my pride.

What can wash away my sins? Nothing but the Blood of Jesus. What can make me whole again? Nothing but the Blood of Jesus.

Sing ye Saints: give voice ye children of God: let the voices of the redeemed sing the glory of the cross, the Blood, the resurrection and the Holy Ghost.

Whilst thou art still in thy flesh, ye Saints, sing of the glory that awaits thee.

It will be worth it all when we see Jesus. Life's trials will seem so small when we see Christ. One glimpse of His dear face, all sorrows will erase. So bravely run the race 'til we see Christ.

Oh that will be glory for me, glory for me, glory for me: when by His grace I shall look on His face; that will be glory: be glory for me.

Sing forth the songs of thy redemption ye people of the Blood: ye that name the name of Jesus, lift up thy voice and sings praises to the Lord.

Psalm 80

I will lift up my voice and give praise to the Lord: His glory and majesty shall I rejoice in.

The Lord is a great and awesome God: let His saints shout His praises in the holy places.

Majesty is thine, O Lord: thy greatness surrounds thy people yet shall we ever delight in the God of our salvation.

The name of the Lord is Holy: powerful and glorious is the name of Jesus the Lord.

Celebrate His glory ye people of the Lord: shout and dance, be glad and exalt the power of His name.

Thou, O Lord, hast a name that is above every name: for it is at the name of Jesus that every knee shall bow and every tongue confess that Jesus Christ is Lord.

The seraphim give praise continually in the throne room of our God: so shall the children of God give honor and praise to His Presence.

The Lord shall forever be exalted by my lips: while I live will I give praise to the Lord and in His Presence in glory shall I exalt His name.

Glorious is the Lord: let the high praises of the Lord abound in His saints.

Though the mountains may leap and the trees clap their hands at the Presence of the Lord so shall the saints of God celebrate His goodness and His love.

Rise up ye children of the Lord and give reverence to His name: in the sanctuaries of the Lord shall His praise be made glorious.

Before the altar of the Lord shall the saints rejoice: in the holy places shall they give praise to the Lord.

Kneel in reverence to His Presence: bow down before the Lord of Glory for He is a great and mighty God: His radiance covers the universe and His glory covers His people as a garment.

O give thanks to the Lord for He is good: His greatness is unsearchable and His power beyond understanding.

Praise the name of the Lord ye people of the Lord: give praise to His name and honor His Presence.

Let the name of Jesus be praised: honor and glory, dominion and power be unto His holy name forever.

Psalm 81

Come Holy Spirit: cover me with thy Presence, O thou great and mighty Spirit of the Most High.

Lord, thou knowest that I need a brand new touch: my strength from yesterday is gone.

Grant me, Holy Spirit, another touch, thus will I have the strength to carry on.

Power of God, consume me: pour out on me thy anointing.

I am weak without thee, O Lord: without thy power I am as a withered blade of grass: as the seeds of the dandelion am I without thy power.

O Lord, my Lord, great and glorious Master of my soul shower thou me with the Holy Ghost and power.

Let the fire of thy Presence burn within me, O God: burn away the dross of my life and let me shine as pure gold before thee: in thy righteousness let me stand before thy Throne.

As living water, flow from me, Almighty Spirit: as water from the Rock in the desert let thy power flood over me and baptize me afresh.

Burn away all that doth not please thee, O Lord: blaze thou within me in living flame.

Allow not thy Presence to smolder, O God, but be thou a conflagration rising up within me for thy glory.

Purge thy servant of all iniquity: let everything within me be as in the Lord Jesus.

Plow up my fallow ground, O God, and let thy Spirit raze all that is infertile.

O thou Spirit of the Sovereign One, consume thy servant: cover thou me with thy holiness, O Lord.

Clothe me, Holy Spirit, with the white robes of thy righteousness that I may be wholly thine, purified by thy holiness and sanctified by thy Presence within me.

Thou hast said, O God, that without holiness no man shall see thee.

O my God, my Lord, my Sustenance, let thy Spirit entirely sanctify me.

Make of me a useful vessel, O God, that in all my doings I shall show forth thy glory to the nations and mirror the image of Jesus to the world.

Devour my soul, Sovereign Spirit: dominate all that is within me.

May I be fully thine, Lord Jesus, that thou, in me, mayest shine forth in radiant glory and that thou mayest be exalted and thy name magnified.

Psalm 82

The sun rises, day begins and I awaken with the praise of the Lord on my lips.

Glory to you, thou great God of Hosts for thou art the Author of the day.

Truly, this is the day that the Lord hath made, I will rejoice and be glad in it.

As the sun rides across the heavens and the winds part the air, the praises of the Lord come flowingly to my heart.

Rise up, O my soul and greet the day. The Lord is thy sustenance and thy support.

By the Spirit of the Lord I live: by the power of His Word do I prosper.

Hours fly: my soul sings. The day progresses: my heart dances.

The Lord is my light and my salvation: The Lord is the joy of my life.

O, Lord, Jesus, how thou hast changed my life: how thou hast brought me up into an high place.

Thou hast loved me with an overwhelming love: thy love hath been shed abroad in my heart by the Holy Ghost.

Thou, O Lord, art my God and my life: without thee I am lost and undone.

By thy power I am as a strong man: as the strength of horses and chariots am I by thy power.

Break forth in singing, O my soul: rise up and rejoice, O my heart. For the Lord thy God is thy buttress and thy stanchion: it is He who hath made thee, yea He hath known thee from the womb and hath called thee into His marvelous light.

Give glory to the Lord when thou riseth, O my soul. Give honor to thy God all day long.

When thou liest down to rest, let the Lord be thy comfort: as the sun goes down may the praise of the Lord be in thy heart and on thy lips.

Praise the Lord, O my soul.

Psalm 83

Thanks be to God for His boundless love: thy love, O Lord hath saved me.

Thanks be to God for His creation: all that is speaks of the glory of the Lord.

Thanks be to God for His redemption: for thou hath taken upon thyself the form of a servant and wast made in the likeness of men.

Thanks be to God for His deliverance: thou hast brought me out of the mirey clay and set my feet upon the Rock.

Thanks be to God for His liberation: thou, O Lord, hast given me release from the chains of my sins and hast given me freedom in Christ Jesus my Lord.

Thanks be to God for His conversion: thou hast made me a new creation.

Thanks be to God for His unspeakable gift: for the gift of God is eternal life through Jesus Christ our Lord.

Thanks be to God for a life in thy family: thou hast grafted me into the beloved and hast made me thy child.

Thanks be to God for the hope of eternity: the assurance of life with thee forever sustaineth my soul.

Thanks be to God for His rescue from death: when I knelt at the cross, my life began at Calvary.

Thanks be to God for His freedom: He whom the Son sets free is free indeed.

Thanks be to God for His liberty: the Lord hath given me free will and my will is thine, O Lord.

Thanks be to God for His sovereignty: thou dost reign in power, O God, and thy greatness is ever before mine eyes.

Thanks be to God for His Spirit: thou hast filled me with thy Spirit and I rejoice in the Holy Ghost.

Thanks be to God for His glory: my heart shall forever give praise unto the Rock of my Salvation.

Thanks be to God for His healing: thou, O Lord, art forever Jehovah-Rapha, the Lord that healeth.

Thanks be to God for His peace: thy peace, O Lord passeth all understanding.

Thanks be to God for His provision: Jehovah-jireh shall forever be my God for He hath given me all things in Christ Jesus.

Thanks be to God for His care and guidance: Thou, O my God shall forever be to me Jehovah-rohi, the Lord my Shepherd.

Thanks be to God for His righteousness: Jehovah-tsidkenu hath clothed me in His righteousness and hath made me into the image of Jesus.

Thanks be to God.

Psalm 84

Hallelujah! Jesus! I praise thee, my Lord.
Glory and honor is thine, great Savior.
Hallelujah, Lord! I love you, Jesus!
Thou art great and mighty. Thou art glorious and holy.
I praise thee, Lord, I praise thee!
Thou hast given me salvation and I praise thee.
Thou hast loved me before I even knew thee and I bless thy name.
Hallelujah! Jesus! Hallelujah, Lord!
Thou art an awesome God. Thou art a wonderful Savior.
Thy blood hath cleansed me. Thy Spirit hath filled me, and I praise thee.
Let my life be praise to thee, Lord Jesus.
Let all that I am, and everything I do give honor and glory to thy name.
Hallelujah, Jesus! Hallelujah!

Psalm 85

Woe to the man that knoweth not the God of Heaven: he shall be as the chaff of wheat and will be blown away in the wind of the judgment.

Woe to the man who denieth the holiness of the Lord of Hosts: his end shall be disaster and torment.

Woe to those that serve false gods, who bow themselves down before idols: they too shall stand before the judgment seat of Christ.

Blessed is the man who walks not in the council of the ungodly: the Lord shall be his sustenance and strength.

Blessed is the man that walketh the road of holiness: the Lord shall reward him with a white robe and crown.

Blessed is the man whose life is lived in the praise of God: he shall have a taste of heaven and his soul shall be satisfied in the Lord His God.

The Lord worketh in all the earth. His reign is sovereign and His glory is eternal.

The eyes of the Lord move to and fro throughout the earth: His hand upholdeth His people but the wicked He will ultimately destroy.

Though there be those that are called gods, they are but the imaginations of man's mind, the working of his hands: they hear not neither doth their ears hear the prayers offered to them.

But the Lord God of Hosts is a mighty God, full of power and might: his arm is not slackened, neither is His strength diminished.

The Lord spoke the universe into existence: His voice flung the stars in place and gave planets their orbits.

Woe to the man who acknowledgeth not the Lord God: they are without excuse for the heavens declare the glory of God and the firmament showeth His handiwork.

Woe to the man who declares in his heart that he hath no need of God: his destiny is sealed by his own heart, he shall endure the torments of hell for his arrogance.

Woe to the man who does despite to the Cross of Christ: for every knee shall bow and every tongue confess that Jesus Christ is Lord.

Blessed is the man who hath washed his garments in the Blood of Jesus: his mansion is assured in heaven and he shall rejoice in the glory of God.

Blessed is the man who gives testimony to the saving power of Christ Jesus: he shall be filled with the Holy Ghost and shall be a joint-heir of God.

Blessed is the man whose God is the Lord: he shall be as a tree planted by rivers of water: he shall prosper in the Lord and shall inherit eternal life.

The works of the Lord are evident in all creation: His power is displayed throughout the universe and His glory is seen in the works of His hands.

The Lord is a God of compassion and mercy: His love endureth forever and His faithfulness is seen throughout all generations.

The Lord is blessed and glorious: His people shall rise up and praise His name for He is a great and awesome God and His people know this right well.

Jesus is Lord over all the earth for He hath been given a name above every name: His people are washed in His Blood and sanctified by His Spirit.

Blessed is the man whose God is the Lord: nothing shall separate him from the love of God that is in Christ Jesus the Lord.

Psalm 86

Lord God of Host, how my soul longeth to give thee praise as thou deserveth.

Yet my tongue is weak, my vocabulary is feeble: my heart rejoices in the Lord and my spirit doth dance in the Presence of the Lord: yet my praise seems ineffective and meager.

The Lord is a great and mighty God: a God of power and might is the Lord Most High.

Thy name, O God shall be praised throughout all the firmament: yea all creation doth shout the glories of their Creator.

How can I praise thee, Lord, more than I have? How can I give thee the adoration that thou deserveth?

My life shall be my praise to thee, O God: in the keeping of thy commandments and the doing of thy will shall I exalt thee.

I shall do all that thou hast spoken, O Lord: my heart shall be thy throne and my spirit shall be thy audience chamber.

In following thee, Lord Jesus, and in keeping and doing they will shall I praise thee: by consecrating my life unto thee and by being filled with thy Spirit shall I show forth my worship of thee, O Lord Jesus, my God.

When my tears fall from mine eyes, may they be even droplets of adoration for thee, O Lord.

When my soul is enraptured in thy Presence let rivers flow from mine eyes that in them I shall glorify the Lord my God.

Let the praise of the Lord be my life goal: let all that is within me strive to glorify the Lord my God.

Let the acclaim of the Lord be my aspiration: let His praise be forever on my lips and demonstrated by my life.

Sanctify me, O God, that I may show unto the nations thy glory that dwelleth within me: Let thy holiness be even as my garments, O God: let me be covered by thy righteousness and thy purity.

Clothe me in thy holiness, O Lord, and let my life be praise unto thee henceforth and forever.

Psalm 87

The Lord is my God: even the God of Abraham, Isaac and Jacob is my God: the Father of my Lord Jesus Christ is my habitation and my refuge: my God in whom I trust.

Rejoice, thou my soul, for thou knowest the Name of thy God: thou knowest the name that is above every name.

There is no God but Jesus: He is magnified in all creation, testified of by the Apostles and Prophets, Himself having become the chief cornerstone.

Rise up, O my soul, and give glory to the Name of Jesus: rejoice thou in the One who wast and is and is to come: all praise and honor to the Name of Jesus!

Glorious art thou, O Lord my Savior: righteous and holy is the Lord Christ.

Thou hast come and wast made in the form of a servant for the suffering of death for all mankind that in thee shall all have the availability of salvation in thee.

Thou hast raised from the dead, O great my Lord and thou art seated at the right hand of the Majesty on High: great is thy name O Jesus, my God.

Thou hast revealed the Father unto us, Lord Jesus, and we have seen in thee that all the fullness dwelt within thee.

By thee doth we have access unto thy Throne room: we may come boldly before the Throne of Grace because thou hast made us acceptable in the beloved.

Shout for joy, all the earth, it is He that hath made us and not we ourselves. We are his people: the sheep of His pasture: He hath shown us His glory by His suffering and His resurrection: and in Him doth we exist in holiness, unto the praise of His glory by Christ Jesus our Lord.

Praised be thou, O Lord.

Let the high praises of the Lord be shouted by the saints: let all that name the name of the Lord dwell in righteousness.

Thou art my God, Lord Jesus, there is none like thee: thou art in all things glorified.

Blessed be the name of the Lord.

Psalm 88

The Lord reigneth: let the people tremble. The Lord dwelleth between the cherubim: let the earth rejoice.

The Lord reigneth: let the children rejoice. The Lord doth ride upon the winds and His footsteps maketh the mountains to quake.

Give unto the Lord high praises: raise up the ram's horn and sound forth the call.

Rise up, ye saints of the Lord and bring forth the sacrifices of praise into the courts of thy God.

The Lord reigneth: let His name be blessed: for the Lord hath set His love upon those that call upon His name, to those that surrender to His salvation by faith. The Lord reigneth: shine forth His glory, ye who art filled with the Holy Ghost: for thy God hath made thee His habitation; yea, the habitation of the Most High are the children of the new covenant.

Praise the name of the Lord, ye who art Blood-bought: shout and rejoice and be glad, ye who have received the forgiveness of sins.

Thy God hath come unto thee, O earth; yea, He hath been born of a virgin and hath found favor in the hearts of His people.

The grave could not hold Him, neither could death keep hold upon Him.

Behold, if that same Spirit dwell in thee that hath raised Christ from the dead, even so shall He quicken thy mortal body by that same Spirit.

The Lord reigneth: pour forth His praise: give unto the Lord the glory due unto His name.

There is none like the Lord: yea, there is none like unto the Lord Jesus for He alone is Lord over all the earth.

All dominion and power hath been given unto Him: give praise to His name. All authority dwelleth within His name: laud Him all ye people.

Let the Spirit arise and revive thy people, O God for we are in need of thee.

Thou art our God and in thee do we trust: thou art our Lord and by thy name are we saved.

The Lord reigneth: sing joyfully unto the Lord: let the high praises of the Lord resound throughout the congregations of the righteous.

The Lord reigneth: let the earth be glad: let the people of the Lord lift up His name in great adoration and acclaim: for the glory of the Lord shall be the habitation of His people and in His Presence shall they receive eternal life.

Psalm 89

Almighty God, how excellent is thy name: thou art a God of power and might: thy majesty is beyond understanding and thy grace beyond compare.

O Lord, my God, thou art an awesome God: full of glory and splendor.

Thou didst speak and the stars were flung into their places: thou knowest all their names.

Thy word went forth and the earth blossomed with fruitfulness and life.

Great is the power of the Lord God of Hosts.

I shall praise thee as long as thou givest me breath: thy praise shall never cease to come from my lips.

Thou art my God and I adore thee: thou art Lord of my life and I worship thee.

Holiness is thy garment and glory doth cover thee as a cloak: thou art clad with righteousness and judgment is thy raiment.

There is none like the Lord God Almighty: His name is written in the hearts of His children: by the name of Jesus shall the children of God be called.

Shower on thy people with thy glory, O God: surround us with thy Presence and let us dwell within thy grace as in a palace.

The Lord Jesus is God above all gods: there is none that can compare to the majesty of the Lord Jesus.

For thou wert born of a virgin, lived amongst men, didst minister unto them the kingdom of God, was crucified, dead and buried: yet thou art risen in glory and doth not remain amongst the dead but liveth forevermore.

Let thy Spirit bring revival to thy people, O God: let those that call upon thy name be enclosed within thy Spirit's power, O Lord.

Spirit of the living God, rise up and consume thy people: let thy church be the habitation of thy Presence by thy Spirit, O Lord Jesus, my Lord and my God.

Let the glory of the Lord arise: let the earth be consumed in thy majesty and thy people within thy Presence.

Make and mold thy people into thine own image, O Lord, that we may be unto thee holiness by thy Word and thy Spirit.

Take those that are thine and make of us a pure Bride adorned with thy righteousness and bedecked in the raiment of holiness: a glorious church without spot or wrinkle, washed in the Blood of the Lamb.

Almighty God, thou art glorious in all thy ways and holy in thy whole being.

Let my soul arise and call thee blessed for the praise of the Lord shall be my covering: the worship of my God as a garment.

Blessed is the Lord Jesus Christ: King and God over all creation: heaven and earth bow before thee, O Lord and thy saints shall praise thy name.

Psalm 90

Thanks be to God for His unspeakable gift: thou hast blessed me with salvation through the Blood of the Lord Jesus the Christ.

Thank be to God for His unspeakable gift: thou hast redeemed me from my sins and hath given me new life.

Thanks be to God for His unspeakable gift: my soul was lost in the mire of iniquity, yea, in iniquity was my soul bound for hell.

Thanks be to God for His unspeakable gift: freedom from sin and life everlasting given by a free gift of God by faith.

Thanks be to God for His unspeakable gift: thou hast provided healing by thy stripes and in the name of Jesus am I healed.

Thanks be to God for His unspeakable gift: by faith in thee I can do all things through Christ that strengthenest me.

Thanks be to God for His unspeakable gift: thou hast anointed me with thy Spirit and in thy Spirit, and by thy name are all things possible.

Thanks be to God for His unspeakable gift: thou hast baptized me in thy Spirit, O God, and hast shed abroad thy love into my heart by the Holy Ghost.

Thanks be to God for His unspeakable gift: the cross hath brought me liberty and in thee I am free from the law of sin and death.

Thanks be to God for His unspeakable gift: thou hast prepared a mansion for me that in thy Presence I may spend eternity worshipping at thy Throne.

Thanks be to God for His unspeakable gift: thou hast given me a heart of praise and my lips shall never cease to praise thee.

Thanks be to God for His unspeakable gift: for nothing is impossible with thee, O Lord, thou hast all power and authority given unto thee for thou hast the name that is above every name.

Thanks be to God for His unspeakable gift: thou art my Provider, in thee I have all I need for thou alone art my God and in thee do I trust all the day.

Thanks be to God for His unspeakable gift: who hast given me the victory through Jesus Christ my Lord.

Psalm 91

Blaze up in me Holy Spirit: let the fire of the Holy Ghost kindle within me.

O Lord, my God, great and mighty One, thou art a God of power and glory: thy people shall rise up and bless thy name forever.

Spirit of the Living God, stir up thy fire that thou mayest burn off all the dross within me. Awaken in me thy power that the nations may see thy power and recognize the might of thy name.

Come, Holy Spirit and work in me: bring forth a conflagration within thy servant that he may show forth thy glory in the sanctuary of the righteous and display thy power to the iniquitous.

O Lord, my Lord, my heart bows before thee for thou and thou alone art God.

There is none like thee, O Lord: my soul rests in thee for thou art my only strength and the lifter of my head.

Thou hast crowned me with thy Spirit, O God, and thou hast made my heart thy habitation: rise up in a blaze, O Spirit, and burn within me.

Let all that is within me be lost in the fire of the Holy Ghost: blaze, Spirit blaze: ignite all of the fullness of the Godhead within me by thy Presence.

Let nothing of me stand in the way of thy fire, O God: take all that is within me and pile it within thine inferno that only thou shalt shine forth from within me and all that is of me be done away with.

Let the beauty of Jesus be seen in me: all His wonderful passion and purity: O, thou Spirit divine, all my nature refine: 'til the beauty of Jesus be seen in me.

Allow naught that is not of thy glory to remain within me: burn away all that is not like Jesus, most Holy Spirit of God.

Create within me a new heart, O God: take away my human heart of stone and give me a heart of flesh that is thine and thine alone.

Raze my humanity: take away my sinful nature and give me a heart towards holiness: reduce to cinders my iniquitous man: leave only ashes to be blown away within the breath of my God.

Take away all that is not of thee, O Lord, and let thy Spirit be within me a blazing fire of holiness unto thee.

Psalm 92

Open mine eyes, O Lord, that I may see as thou doth see: that mine eyes may behold the plight of the lowly and the needs of the weary.

Thou, O Lord, art ever mindful of the needy: thy heart doth encompass those of low estate.

Let me not see iniquity that surroundeth me but let me see those in poverty and those that may be destitute.

The Lord is the source of all: His hand is open to the weak and His strength is given to those that call upon His name in faith.

Be thou my vision, O Lord of my life: show me those in need that thy Gospel may be given unto them and that they might see the riches of thy glory in Christ Jesus.

The Lord giveth strength to the weary and help to the needy: they shall call upon the Lord and He shall raise them up to new heights of splendor.

The Lord is high and holy: there is none like Him: yet hath he regard for the oppressed and His hand is extended to the broken.

Behold the lilies of the field, they toil not, neither do they spin, but the Lord hath regard for them.

The eyes of the Lord roam to and fro throughout all the earth: He sees the sparrow when it falls and knoweth all the stars by their names.

The Lord is a mighty God: all power and glory is due unto His name.

Help thou me, O Lord that in thy name I may extend a cup of cool water: let the beauty of Jesus be seen in me.

Let me not regard iniquity, neither let me have knowledge of the sinful: but let me see their need of thee that thy Word may come forth and bring victory to those who are oppressed by wickedness.

Bring down injustice, O God, for thou art a holy Judge and in righteousness doth thou meet out thy judgments.

Let me not be haughty, O God: let not my soul be lifted up in pride.

Let me see as thou doth see, O God, and let thy Spirit be my guide in all things to the honor and glory of thy name.

Psalm 93

Let my heart be thy temple, O Lord, my God: dwell thou within me even as thou didst in the temple of Solomon.

Let the glory cloud descend upon me as in the consecration of the temple: pour out upon me thy Spirit that I may be thy true habitation.

Take from me all that displeaseth thee, O Lord, that I may be sanctified to thy purpose alone: purge me of all that is not wholly consecrated to thy service and thy will.

Make my life a living sacrifice, holy and acceptable in thy sight, O Lord my Rock and my Redeemer.

Thou hast said that thou doest desire obedience rather than sacrifice: let mine obedience to thy Word, thy Will and thy purpose be my complete sacrifice unto thee: may my life be a sweet savor before thee, O Lord.

The Lord dwelleth not in a sanctuary made with hands: in a temple of flesh doth the Lord desire to dwell. In the hearts of the consecrated, the souls of the surrendered, the lives of the sanctified doth the Lord seek to make His habitation.

Neither the blood of sheep nor bulls shall satisfy the Lord: in a clean heart, a surrender spirit and a sanctified life shall the Lord take pleasure.

Let all that is within me be unto thee a sweet savor: may the incense of my surrender to thee be pleasant in thy nostrils, O Lord my God.

Take all of me and sanctify me as thy dwelling: cover me with the gold of thy Spirit and purify me within and without, that all of me may be unto thee a Throne and a residence for thy purpose and glory.

Even as thou didst dwell in Jerusalem and even as thy House wast amongst thy people in the midst of Zion, so, Lord, dwell thou within me: make thy servant thine abode and make my life thy lodging: my heart thy temple in sanctity.

May all my life be the place of thy worship: a shrine of holiness shall I be unto thee, O Lord, if thou wilt indwell me with thy Spirit and make me thy Holy Place: let my heart be thy Holy of Holies, O Lord, my God and my Savior.

As thou didst sacrifice thyself for me upon the cross, even so shall my life be a continual sacrifice for thee and a holy place for thy dwelling.

Let thy servant be thy temple, O God: let my heart be thy Throne and my life thy holy habitation through Jesus Christ my Lord and my God.

Psalm 94

O Lord, I cry unto thee: hear thou my prayer, O God.

Turn not thine ear from me, O Lord: listen to the call of thy servant.

My petition I lay before thy throne, O thou Holy One: turn not away from me, O my God.

O Lord, thou art my strength: in thee is my sustenance and supply.

Hear the cry of my heart, O God: thy servant calleth to thee for thou alone art a God of power who knoweth all my ways and my heart.

I have no strength but in thee, O God: Lord Jesus, my God, hear me as I call unto thee: turn not away from me but hear me as I call upon thy name.

The wicked have no strength: there is no sustenance in them neither do they have any to uphold them.

But the Lord is a God who is sensitive to His people: yea, the Lord knoweth the course He hath set for those that love Him; to those that are called by His name.

Stretch forth thy hand, O God, and do what only thou canst do: thou knowest my plight: thou knowest the needs of thy servant.

Attend to my voice, O Lord, as I call upon thee: Lord Jesus, be thou my refuge as I turn to thee in my need.

Ignore not my plea, O God: examine my heart and see that it is turned to thee in faith and in confidence.

Consider the call of thy servant, O Lord, and give ear to my heart's cry.

There is none but thee, Lord, that canst rescue thy servant: turn not from me.

Take notice of my heart, O thou my God and hear the voice of my petition as I call upon thy name, Lord Jesus.

O Lord, I trust in thee: thou art my God and in thee do I trust.

The Lord my God, my Savior and King is Jesus the Christ: there is none like unto the Lord of Hosts.

Thou knowest when a sparrow falls and thou dost call all the stars by name: there is no power in any but the Lord God Almighty.

Thy power and thy strength, O God is unsearchable: thou hast more strength than my mind canst comprehend.

In thee, do I trust O God: hear thou my call and be thou the supplier of my need according to thy riches in glory by Christ Jesus.

Psalm 95

O God, thou art my God and I will ever praise thee: thou art my Savior and I will glorify thy name throughout my life.

Let my life be a praise to thee, O Lord: let all that is within me praise thy holy name.

Thou didst call forth Lazarus from the grave: thy power was seen in his coming forth.

Thou didst calm the raging sea of Galilee: thy might was witnessed by thy voice stilling the storm.

It was thy hand that didst spread mud on the eyes of the blind man: his eyes being opened showed forth thy glory.

O Lord, thou art great and mighty: glorious and holy art thou, Lord Jesus my God.

Strength and honor, dominion and power be unto thy name, O God: thou art the sustainer of creation and by thy will doth all that exists continue.

Praise be unto thee, O Lord Jesus Christ: praise and honor be unto thy name.

For thy name, O Lord is above every name: thy power is spread forth throughout the earth by thy name.

Thou didst bless the loaves and fishes and didst feed five thousand men: women and children also did eat by the provision of thy power, O Lord.

Thy hand didst touch the lepers and make them whole: their bones and skin renewed by the power of thy touch, O God.

A single touch of the fringe of thy prayer shawl didst dry up the issue of blood: the women sick for twelve years was cured by her faith in thy power.

Glorious is the Lord God Almighty, Maker of heaven and earth, sustainer of all, and Lord of my life.

Praise be unto thee, O Lord: let the name of Jesus be praised throughout the earth.

Let all thy saints give praise to thee, O Lord: let thy saints glory in thy Presence by the Spirit, O thou King of the Universe.

Lift up thy voice, O my soul and sing praise to the Lord: let the words of my mouth and the meditations of my heart be acceptable in thy sight, O Lord my Rock and my Redeemer.

Rise up ye saints and bless the Lord: let the redeemed of the Lord shout forth His glory: let the Blood-bought give voice to the majesty of the Lord.

As for me, I will ever give praise unto thee, O Lord, for thou art the God of the Universe, yet Lord of my life: my Redeemer art thou, O thou Bethlehem-born King.

The Lord is glorious beyond description: none there be that can give forth the praises due unto the name of Jesus: Yet with my life I will bless the Lord: with my voice will I praise thee, O thou Most High.

Psalm 97

Thy grace, O God, doth sustain me: thou hast upheld me by thy Word and hath saved me by thy grace.

There is no one like the Lord my God: thou art alone in thy power, O God.

The Lord is full of mercy and wondrous in power: the Lord shows mercy to the merciful and His power is seen throughout the universe.

This poor soul called upon the Lord and He heard me out of His holy Hill and poured out His grace upon me bringing me into His full and free salvation through faith.

Great is the mercy of the Lord: His love is shed abroad in our hearts by the Holy Ghost.

The people of the Lord are a people showered with grace: His Spirit called, faith responded and grace hath brought forth salvation.

O that men would turn to the Lord and seek His face: turn to the Lord while He may be found for His wrath shall not be held back forever, neither shall His judgment be kept back indefinitely.

The Word of the Lord is sure: His faithfulness is certain and His grace is abundant.

The Lord hath spoken and He shall do it: nothing of the Word of the Lord shall not come to pass.

Woe to those that disregard the Word of the Lord: they shall be as the grass of the field: they shall wither and burn in the power of His wrath.

They shall be trodden down and destroyed because they have ignored the warnings of God's Word.

The righteous rejoice in the statues of the Lord: His Word brings enlightenment to their hearts and joy to their souls.

Strong in might shall be the people of the Book: they have planted themselves in the garden of God's Word and His voice brings forth growth and strength within them.

The Lord blesses those that hide His Word in their hearts for they might not sin against the Lord.

The God of Glory hath spoken: His Word is recorded: blessed is the man that trusteth in the Word of the Lord.

Psalm 98

I will praise the Lord while I live: from my moment of rising until I lay me down to rest, the praise of the Lord shall flow forth from my lips.

I will glorify the Lord as long as I live: my life shall be my worship of my God.

Sing to the Lord, O heart of mine: break forth in shouting O my soul: for the Lord thy God hath redeemed thee: He hath brought thee out of sin and hath made thee a new creation in Christ Jesus.

Therefore will I praise the Lord: He hath done bountifully with me: His grace hath brought me salvation through His blood and by faith in His atonement.

Glory in the Lord, O my soul: give praise unto the King of Heaven for His love hath bought thee: yea, His sacrifice hath redeemed thee.

My lips shall speak forth the praises of the Lord: my soul shall not cease to praise my Lord for He hath brought me out of the mire and hath given unto me His Spirit: for which I shall forever glory in the Lord. Praised be His name.

Shout to the Lord, O heart within me: give praise to His name and bow down before His holy Throne.

For the Lord is the King of Heaven: He hath laid the foundations of the earth and by His will doth the earth spin in its orbit.

The sun and moon are in their courses by the order of the Lord: He hath spoken and they obey.

The stars hath He flung into the cosmos: yea, He hath called them all by name: His knowledge is unsearchable.

The planets hath He ordered: none of them leaveth their orbit for the Lord hath laid out their course.

Fly ye comets for thy tails flair forth in praise of thy Creator: burn, O sun, for thy heat doth proclaim the matchlessness of God.

Shine forth ye stars and twinkle thou in worship of the Lord Almighty.

Wax and wane, O moon, for the Lord hath given thee light and thy cycle hath been set by the Word of His mouth.

Rise up ye seas and crash forth the praises of God: blow forth ye winds in worship of the Almighty One.

If I praise not the Lord my God the rocks shall cry out the majesty of the Lord.

While I live will I praise my God and whilst breath is within me shall I speak forth the glory of the redemption of my God.

Praise the Lord, O my soul: and forget not all His benefits for He hath done mighty things within thee and hath given thee eternal life through Jesus Christ thy Lord.

Psalm 99

Thy joy, O God doth uphold me: tempests may blow, storms may come but the joy of the Lord is continually with me.

Nothing can come against me to destroy the joy that cometh by thy salvation, O Lord: thou hast given thy Blood and in that Blood doth my soul rejoice.

O my soul, be thou comforted by the joy of thy God: His Spirit hath possessed thee and by His Spirit shalt thou ever rejoice and be glad.

In myself I am nothing: there is no good within me apart from my God.

The Lord hath raised me up and hath made me to be a partaker of His blessings in the beloved and in this shall I ever rejoice..

Rage ye storms. Blow ye winds. Cast forth thy gale. Nothing shall separate me from the love of God that is in Christ Jesus the Lord.

My soul shall ever give praise to the Lord for His manifest blessing: the Lord is my strength and my sure tower of security.

Naught shall come against me that shall take my joy: hear, O my soul and be glad in the faithfulness of the Lord thy God.

Thy Word is a light unto my path and in thy Word doth my soul rejoice: the law of the Lord is a glory to mine heart and a blessing to my soul.

In the Lord doth I glory: my soul shall ever bless the name of the Holy One and in His service shall I find fulfilling joy.

Though the enemy shall cast commotion towards me; though turmoil shall rampage and roar around me yet shall I stand on the Rock of my salvation and give glory to the Holy One who giveth me joy in the morning.

No disturbance shall dismay me nor any uproar cause me to wince; for the Lord hath made me His habitation, yea, He hath filled me with His Spirit and by His power, in the name of Jesus, I am blessed beyond the curse.

Praise the Lord, O my soul and give glory to the Rock of thy salvation. Bless the Lord and praise His name for He hath done marvelous things unto thee.

Psalm 100

The Lord is an amazing God: His power is unsearchable and His greatness beyond understanding.

The Lord doth reign in heaven and the earth is His footstool.

The greatness of the Lord is glorious: mighty and strong is the Lord God Almighty.

For the love of His creation hath the great God of Heaven taken the form of a servant and was made in the likeness of men.

The love of the Lord is shed abroad in the hearts of His saints by His Spirit: mighty is the Lord.

Jesus shall reign over all the earth: all things are given into His power and nothing remains that is not under His hand.

The sun doth shine as praise to the Lord of Hosts: the moon reflects its glory and doth show forth the majesty of the Lord.

From the rising of the sun to the going down of the same, the name of the Lord is to be praised.

Shine forth ye stars in worship of the Lord: let thy brilliance give forth His praises.

The Lord is God: there is none like Him.

By His word doth all exist: nothing that is was brought about but by the word of the Lord.

Give praise to His name ye saints: quake and tremble ye wicked for the Lord sitteth in judgment and His righteousness shall He uphold.

The nations shall see His glory: all peoples shall know the glory of the Lord.

For the trumpet shall sound and the dead shall be raised incorruptible.

The voice of the Archangel shall give forth his word and the ram's horn of the Lord shall sound.

Naught can withstand the coming of the Lord: He shall conquer the earth in righteousness and rule the nations in holiness and justice.

All the earth shall give forth the praises of the Lord Jesus: for He shall return as He hath said.

Give praise to His name and bless the Lord all ye His saints.

Shout forth the glory of the Lord and make known His holiness.

Psalm 101

O Lord, our Lord, how excellent is thy name in all the earth.

Heaven and earth doth testify to the majesty of the Lord God of Hosts: his glory is excellent and His mercy endureth forever.

The name of the Lord hath been highly exalted: the name of Jesus is above every name that is named.

By thy name, O Lord, the dumb hath speech: they shall proclaim the greatness of thy name.

Behold, how God anointed Jesus of Nazareth with the Holy Ghost and with power: who went about doing good, and healing all that were oppressed of the devil.

Thy name, O God, thou blessed Jesus, hath opened the eyes of the blind: they shall see thee when thou returnest for the power of thy name hath given them sight.

The name of the Lord is a strong and mighty tower: the righteous run into it and are saved.

How glorious is thy name, Lord Jesus? There is untold power in thy name, thou Lord Christ.

The bound and oppressed are set free at the mention of thy name: when they call upon thee with faith in thy name they are liberated by thy power.

Great is the Lord and greatly to be praised.

There is none like our God; yea, none can compare to the glory of the Lord Jesus for He hath conquered death, hell and the grave and hath risen victorious unto new life: behold, he doth live forever and of His kingdom there shall be no end.

Give unto the Lord the glory due unto His name: for the Lord Jesus the Christ hath a name exalted above every name.

By thy name, O God, shall every knee bow and every tongue confess that Jesus Christ is Lord.

Demons tremble at the mention of thy name, Lord Jesus: at thy name they shall quake in fear and be banished.

There is salvation in no other name than the name of Jesus: no man cometh unto the Father but by Him.

Leap with joy ye lame for by the name of Jesus hath their limbs received new health and hath been made whole.

Diseases are healed by faith in the name of Jesus: behold, His power is resident in His name and none shall there be that cannot reach out to Him by their faith.

The Lord hath spoken and His Word is verity: In my name shall they cast out devils; they shall speak with new tongues; They shall take up serpents; and if they drink any deadly thing, it shall not hurt them; they shall lay hands on the sick, and they shall recover: this is the Word of the Lord who cannot lie.

There is power in thy name, O Lord: great and mighty is the name of Jesus.

Thy God hath provided for thee health and security by His Blood: by His stripes ye are healed.

Trust in the Lord with all thine heart and lean not unto thine own understanding: in all thy ways acknowledge Him and He shall direct thy path.

Have faith in the name of Jesus, ye who suffer in pain.

Ye who have need of healing call upon the name of the Lord Jesus Christ: for by the power of the name of Jesus Christ of Nazareth are diseases healed and lives made new.

Glorious and mighty is thy name, O Lord: Blessed shalt thou be forever. Amen.

Psalm 102

How glorious is the Lord of Hosts: how majestic is his name.

The Lord deals bountifully with his people: with those that are His doth He shed forth His grace and doth save them to the uttermost.

The Lord, the great God, is a mighty God full of compassion to those that call upon His name: to those that call upon Him in faith and confidence.

The Holy One doth show Himself glorious in His creation: in the works of His hands doth He show forth His power.

There is none like the Lord of Heaven: the Holy One reigneth in righteousness and in great power doth He proclaim His sovereignty.

Who can know the glory of the Lord? Who can understand His power?

Those that come to Him in faith: to them doth He display His glory. To those that call upon the name of Jesus doth they receive the understanding of His power.

The Lord is the way, the truth, and the life, no man cometh to the Father but by Him.

There is no God but the Lord Jesus: there is none that can match His power and glory.

Those that are called gods are false and powerless: they are the dumb imaginations of the mind of man.

Behold how abundant is the love of God towards those that are His children: to those that call upon His name doth His shed forth His love by the Holy Ghost.

Glorious and holy, righteous and mighty is the Lord: majestic and sovereign is He.

The Lord is full of mercy and willing in grace: He giveth to all that call upon Him in faith.

The Lord showeth His mercy to the poor: to the desolate doth He display His compassion.

He doth clothe the lilies of the field: the sparrows are fed by His hand.

He calleth the stars by their names: The Lord hath the hairs of thy head numbered.

There is no limit to the power of the Lord God Almighty: neither is there any confinement to His glorious might.

He is and was mighty in His person: He is overwhelmingly powerful and nothing is hidden from Him.

The Lord is God: Jesus is His name and before His name shall all knees bow and all tongues confess that He alone is Lord of all forever.

Psalm 103

Praise ye the Lord. I will praise the Lord with my whole heart, in the assembly of the upright, and in the congregation.

Before the people of the Lord will I give unto my God the praises of my heart.

The Lord is upright and just, his commandments are truth and verity and in His hand is the rod of judgment.

He gives to the poor their needs and brings to the weary new strength.

When I stand in the sanctuary of the Lord I shall lift up my voice and give praise to the God of my salvation.

To the Lord Jesus the Christ shall I forever give praise and honor; unto the Lord will I give glory.

Praise ye the Lord, ye people of the Lord. In the dwelling place of the Lord lift up thy hands unto the name of Jesus and bless His name.

Though the meek shall inherit the earth, yet shall only the Blood-bought inherit eternal life through Jesus Christ our Lord.

Holy and upright is the Lord of Hosts. His name is glorious and worthy of praise.

Sing unto the Lord and be glad ye children of the Lord: give honor and praise to His name for He alone hath dominion over all things.

Power is held in His hand and by His voice was the universe created.

Glory shineth from His eyes and lightning doth blaze from His countenance.

Give unto the Lord the glory due unto His name for He is a great and mighty God and worthy of all praise.

Lift up your voice ye daughters of the Church: raise ye a tumult of worship to the Lord thy God.

Break forth in praise ye sons of the Covenant: shout and rejoice in thy salvation through the Blood.

Praise ye the Lord. His work is honorable and glorious and His righteousness endureth forever.

Holy is the Lord and in holiness shall His people worship His name.

The Lord hath called His people to dwell in His righteousness and by His Spirit doth He shower them with His holiness.

Praise ye the Lord. Praise Him and glorify His name: for He hath done marvelous things. In His Presence is fullness of joy. Praise ye the Lord.

Psalm 104

In the weary and barren land I will bless the Lord.

Through the storms of life shall my heart give glory to the Lord.

In the midst of mine enemies and in the face of great trouble shall I lift up my voice in praise to the Lord.

The Lord is worthy of all praise: His name is glorious and there is no limit to His power.

Though the enemy shall strike me; though my strength shall fail me, yet will I praise my God.

In the congregation of righteous will I sing praises: in the dwelling place of my God shall I ever lift up my voice in glory.

Though I may walk in the wilderness of despair, or dwell in the desert of despondency, yet will my soul praise the Lord.

Though my way may seem fraught will hopelessness, or my spirit may lag in anguish, even so shall I give praise to the Lord and His glory shall be the lifter of my head.

I am victorious in the Lord my God through the Blood of Calvary.

Though gloom may cast a shadow over me, even so shall I glory in the cross.

I shall not lose heart for the Lord hath brought me victory through His sacrifice.

In the Lord am I raised up. In the Lord am I triumphant.

Nothing shall come against me that is not seen by the eye of the Almighty.

Nothing shall come against me that I cannot conquer through the Blood of the Lamb and the word of my testimony.

In the barrenness of life I may wander through my days, but yet, I know, that this world is not my Home: neither am I a citizen of this country for my citizenship is in Heaven by the power and glory of the cross of the Lord Jesus.

I shall dwell in the wonders of my God and in His holiness shall I ever rejoice.

My days may seem dreary but in the Lord am I champion.

In the face of trouble shall I bless the Lord: in anxiety or care shall I praise my God.

My victory is in Jesus and by His Spirit shall I dwell in holiness and bless the Lord through the length of my days. Bless the name of the Lord.

Psalm 105

Praise ye the Lord. Praise, O ye servants of the Lord, praise the name of the Lord.

Blessed be the name of the Lord from this time forth and for evermore.

From the rising of the sun unto the going down of the same the Lord's name is to be praised.

Forever shall the Lord be glorified: the praise of His name shall never cease.

Lift up thy voice, ye servants of the Lord, and give Him glory.

The Lord is a gracious God, a righteous King and a glorious sovereign.

To the name of the Lord shall His people give praise: unto God shall the righteous rejoice in His holiness.

Bless the Lord, O my soul and forget not all His benefits.

Lift up your voice, O my soul: give glory to the Lord for His mercy and grace.

The Lord hath provided salvation through the cross and by His Blood hath He provided deliverance.

Praise ye the Lord. Blessed is the man that feareth the Lord, that delighteth greatly in his commandments.

His seed shall be mighty upon earth: the generation of the upright shall be blessed.

Give praise to the Lord ye Blood-bought: to the God of thy salvation give praise.

The Lord is abundant in His mercy, yet in righteousness shall He judge the nations.

All shall see the glory of the Lord: His return shall be in power and glory and every knee shall bow to the name of the Lord Jesus.

The praise of the Lord shall be the banner of the saved: the standard of holiness shall be raised high by those washed in the Blood of the Lamb.

The sun shall rise and the moon continue on its course in the heavens: day after day shall the righteous bless the name of the Lord.

O praise the Lord all ye nations: praise Him all ye people.

The Lord hath done marvelous things and in His power shall He lift up His people and bring them into His kingdom by His might.

Sin hath been removed: death hath been conquered in the name and by the power of the Lord.

Jesus hath been lifted up, yet before all the nations shall He be glorified.

Of His kingdom there shall be no end: Jesus shall reign over all the earth and all peoples shall call Him blessed.

Give praise to the Lord ye people of the Lord: to the name of the Holy One give praise.

Psalm 106

Give glory to His name: the name above all names.

Give glory and praise to the name of Jesus: His name is Wonderful.

Ascribe unto the Lord majesty and honor: the name of Jesus is Counselor.

Rise up, ye people of the Lord and praise His name: His name is glorious before all the gods.

The name of the Lord is holy: above the heavens is the glory of his name.

Praise and honor, glory and power be unto the name of the Lord: Dominion is His and might is abundant in the name of Jesus.

The Mighty God is He: Jesus is the Prince of Peace and of His Kingdom there shall be no end.

Arise ye children of God and bless His name: for the name of Jesus is exalted in heaven and on earth and His glory is unspeakable.

The angels cease not to cry holy, holy before His Throne for He is glorious beyond description.

The Lord hath conquered death, hell and the grave: before His name demons tremble and quake.

Bless the Lord O ye congregation of the righteous: unto His name give praise in the sanctuary.

Lift up thy hands in the name of Jesus and cry forth His majesty throughout the earth.

Let the voices of the Blood-washed shout out the glory of the King of Kings.

Come before His Presence with boldness, ye people of the Lord, and give Him praise: for He hath bought thee with a price and thou art adopted into His family by the Blood of Jesus.

Let the saints bow before His Throne and give Him glory: apostles and prophets give forth the praises of the Lord.

He is the Everlasting Father: His love hath been displayed on Calvary and unto all that call upon Him in faith doth His shed forth His grace.

Give glory to His name: Jesus the Christ be praised: glory to the Lord God of Heaven.

Psalm 107

The name of the Lord is a strong and mighty tower: let His praise be glorious.

He rides upon the winds and the lightening flashes at His command: let His praise be glorious.

The universe is His throne room and the earth is His footstool: let His praise be glorious.

By the voice of the Most High the stars were flung into space: let His praise be glorious.

The planets and moons were set in their orbits by His word: let His praise be glorious.

The Lord is full of compassion and His mercy endureth forever: let His praise be glorious.

Speak His praises and give forth His glory for the Lord thy God hath chosen thee from the inhabitants of the earth and hath adopted thee into His family through the Blood of the cross of Christ.

The mountains tremble at the footsteps of the Lord: let His praise be glorious.

The waves crash upon the rocks by the command of the Lord: let His praise be glorious.

The seas rage and the tumult is raised by the will of the Almighty: let His praise be glorious.

The Lord doth judge in righteousness; His judgments are verity and truth: let His praise be glorious.

The great God of heaven is holy and just. In righteousness shall He bring the nations to Him: let His praise be glorious.

The people of the Lord shall give voice to His praises in the sanctuary in His Presence: let His praise be glorious.

They shall lift up holy hands in worship of His glory: let His praise be glorious.

The Blood-bought shall lift up their voices and shout unto the God of their salvation: let His praise be glorious.

The Lord is love and He hath displayed His affection for His people at the cross: let His praise be glorious.

Great is the Lord and great is His name: let His praise be glorious.

Great is the Lord, He is holy and just: by His mercy we trust in His love: let His praise be glorious.

The sparrows are fed by the hand of His grace: let His praise be glorious.

The lilies of the field find their growth through the will of the Most High: let His praise be glorious.

The corn and the wheat grow by His will: let His praise be glorious.

The new wine is brought upon the vine: let His praise be glorious.

All that doth grow upon the earth has its roots in the will of the Lord: let His praise be glorious.

Nothing that exists came into being but by the voice of God: let His praise be glorious.

The worlds were made and the universe came into being by the word of the Lord God of Hosts: let His praise be glorious.

Sin was conquered and all trespasses removed by the Blood of Jesus: let His praise be glorious.

The cross of Calvary showed forth the love of God: let His praise be glorious.

The empty grave showed thc power of His might: let His praise be glorious.

Death, hell, and the grave were put under His feet: let His praise be glorious.

All power is in the name of the Lord Jesus of Hosts: let His praise be glorious.

Captain of the Armies of heaven is He: let His praise be glorious.

He reigns in heaven and the inhabitants of the earth shall become His servants: let His praise be glorious.

Who can speak the praises of the Lord or give to His name the glory that He is due? The Lord is glorious beyond the understanding of man and His holiness is a banner held high by the righteous.

O, that I might have a thousand tongues to be able to speak forth the praises of the Lord Jesus for He hath done mighty deeds.

Year upon year and ten thousand times ten thousands of years shall not be enough to give forth the praises that are in my heart to the Lord my Savior.

The Lord is high and holy: let His praise be glorious.

The Lord is mighty to deliver all that call upon His name: let His praise be glorious.

To those that lift up their faith unto His majesty the Lord is continually faithful: let His praise be glorious.

There is no one like unto the Lord. None there be that can outshine His glory: let His praise be glorious.

Glory to the Lord; Praise, honor, worship, dominion, power, and majesty be unto the God of Heaven, the Lord Jesus the Christ: let His praise be glorious.

Psalm 108

Hear thou me, O God: let not thine ears be closed to my voice, O thou Holy One.

I call upon thee in my need, O Lord, hear me.

Thou and thou alone art able to give me help, O my God.

I cry unto thee, for thou art my Father and in thee do I put all my trust.

In my distress I call upon thee, O Lord, for I know that thou dost hear me and art able to do exceedingly abundantly above anything that I could ask or think, by thine own power in the name of Jesus.

Turn not away from me in mine anguish: turn not thy face away from me in my difficulty.

Thou knowest me, O Lord: thou knowest my heart and seest all that in within me.

Thou dost know, O God, that I am thine: I have been washed in the Blood of Calvary and thou hast made me the habitation of thy Spirit.

My soul is in misery, O Lord: unto thee do I lift up my voice. Hear me, O Lord my God.

My suffering hath brought me low: but the Lord is my strength and in thee do I have full confidence.

Thou art righteous, O God, and faithful to thy children: therefore do I raise my voice before thee for thou art able to rescue me from my trouble.

Hear me, O God, that I may stand in testimony of thy mercy towards thy servant.

I call upon thee in Jesus' name knowing that thou dost always hear me when I call.

Liberate me, O Lord, from my distress: release me from my troubles by thy power, O thou Most High.

My heart is in sadness yet will I praise thee, O Lord: I will ever give praise unto thee, thou my God for thou art worthy of all praise.

Though my soul may go down to the pit, yet shall I praise the Lord: though I may find myself in the depths of Sheol, even so with my last breath I shall give praise unto thee, O Lord.

Hear me, O God: let not thine ears be closed to the voice of my petitions, in Jesus' name.

Psalm 109

O Lord my God, how can I give thee more praise?

How can my heart be lifted more fully before thee in honor?

Thou art worthy, O God, of all glory and praise. Thou art the most glorious God; Maker of heaven and earth.

How can my voice give thee more worship?

How can my tongue speak forth more of thy praise?

Thou dost sit on the Throne of Heaven and by thy word doth the universe exist.

By thy word wert the stars flung into place: thy voice didst speak worlds into existence.

When I think of Calvary my soul doth rise in praise to thee, O God.

When I consider thy sacrifice in pain and agony for my sake, my voice cries in thanksgiving to thee, O Lord.

Thy Blood hath washed my sins away: thy Blood hath brought me nigh to thy Throne.

Thou didst bleed and die that I might have life and have it more abundantly and I praise thee, O my Lord.

Thy love didst take thee to Calvary and to the tomb: in power didst thou rise from the dead to sit at the right hand of the Majesty on high.

O that I could give thee adequate praise, O God: O that my voice was a choir glorifying thy name.

Thou art worthy, O God: adoration and praise is thine.

Honor and glory, praise, exaltation, power, dominion, and might is due unto thy name, O thou Holy One, Lord of Hosts.

In gratitude doth my heart bow before thee, O Lord.

In worship is my soul lifted up in adoration of thy glory.

Thou art majestic, O God, above all that are called gods: in vain do they receive laud from those that bow down before them.

How can I praise thee more fully, O God?
How can I worship thee more deeply?
Thou art my God and my desire is to praise thy most holy name forever and ever.

Psalm 110

When I survey the wondrous cross, on which the Prince of Glory died, my richest gain I count but loss and pour contempt on all my pride.

Thy cross, O God, is my place of refuge.

In tears do I contemplate thy sacrifice for me.

Behold mine eyes doth flow with gratitude and praise when I look upon the cross and doth think of thee.

Thy love didst bring thee to Golgotha and in misery and anguish didst thou lay down thy life for me.

Thou didst suffer arrest and prosecution for my sins: for the sins of thy created ones didst thou face judgment.

Thy face wast slapped, yea thy beard did they pluck out: thou wert humiliated for my transgressions.

In vainglory did they put a crown of thorns upon thy holy brow and didst mock thee in regal robes.

Thou wert beaten and flogged that my diseases might be healed: thy body didst receive stripes for my healing.

In love didst thou carry the cross beam to the hill where thy love didst bring thee to Calvary.

They didst strip off thy clothing: yea, they did gamble for thy robe: for thy garments didst they cast lots.

Naked wert thou hung before the world on the cross: thy blessed hands and feet wert pierced by nails: thou wert hung upon a tree for mine iniquity.

O Lord, thou didst suffer in anguish for me: thy body wast broken and beaten for me.

For love of thy creation didst thou willing give thyself in sacrifice.

For love of the works of thy hands didst thou give thy blood and thy life.

How can I not bow in repentance and honor before thee, O thou my Lord?

How can I not praise thee for what thou hast done for me at Calvary?

Yet, even as thou didst die, yet the grave couldst not hold thee: death could not maintain its hold on thee: for thou didst conquer death, hell, and the grave and thou art alive forevermore.

Thou art alive and thou doth reign in my heart, O God: because of Calvary thou hast purchased my redemption: by thy Blood am I redeemed.

Behold how my tears doth worship thee, O Lord: behold how my weeping doth give thee praise.

When I think of the cross and all that thou hast done for me, I worship thee, O Lord.

Thou hast made me nigh by the Blood of the cross and in adoration doth my heart bow before thee and call thee Blessed.

When I think of thine agony, O Lord, my soul doth weep in gratitude.

When I think of the love that took thee to the cross, in appreciation doth my soul rise up in praise before thee, O Lord.

Jesus, my Lord, my God, and my Sovereign, thou didst love me with an overwhelming love: thy love didst bring thee to Golgotha and thy power didst raise thee from the tomb.

Jesus, thy name is power. Jesus, thy name is might. Jesus, thy name will break every stronghold. Jesus, thy name is life.

O Lord I praise thee: O my God I give thee mine whole heart as thy throne.

Reign thou in me, O God, for thy name, Lord Jesus, is the glory of thy power; yea, all that is the might of thy godhead in within thy name, O Lord.

Thou hast bought me with a price: the price of thy precious Blood hath purchased me.

I am thine, O Lord, I have heard thy voice and it told thy love to me.

Consecrate me now to Thy service, Lord, by the power of grace divine; Let my soul look up with a steadfast hope, and my will be lost in thine.

Let not mine eyes cease to flow with tears when I think of the cross: let not my weeping end when I consider thy suffering for me.

I will bow before thee in worship, O Lord: for thou hast brought me to thee by thy pain, yea by thy Blood hath thou drawn me to thy side.

Thy Blood hath made me free: thy Blood hath released me from mine iniquity and from my transgressions didst thou redeem me.

O my soul, be thou lifted up in thy God for He hath given thee life by the cross and eternity is thine by the empty tomb.

King of my life, I crown thee now, thine shall the glory be. Lest I forget thy thorn crowned brow, lead me to Calvary. Lest I forget Gethsemane, lest I forget thine agony, lest I forget thy love for me, lead me to Calvary.

My soul shall ever praise thee, Lord Jesus, and in thy name shall I go forth into the world and proclaim thy love and grace: by the power of thy Spirit shall I ever declare the glory of thy name for Calvary covers it all and my praise is thine, O Lord, forever and ever more.

Psalm 111

Glory and honor, wisdom and power be unto the Ancient of Days.

Majesty and power, magnificence and splendor be unto the Ancient of Days.

Lift your voices ye children of God: raise thine instruments and play music to the glory of His name: for the Lord thy God is awesome in might and glorious in His strength.

Admiration and laud, worship and devotion be unto the Ancient of Days.

The Lord is a God of righteousness: in his hand is the balance of justice.

Truth is His garment and with holiness is He clothed.

The Lord God of Heaven is merciful and gracious: with love He doth compass about His people and as a Shepherd doth He lead them in His ways.

There is no one like our God: yea, there is no one like unto His glory.

Holiness is His robe, it doth surround Him and cover Him and in His holiness doth He present Himself to His people by His Spirit.

Give thanks to the Lord for His love and His mercy: give thanks to His name and give Him praise.

Show forth thy devotion to the Lord of Hosts for He hath done marvelous things, and it is wondrous in our eyes and glorious to behold.

Worship the Lord in the beauty of holiness: let His sanctifying power consume thee as thou dost magnify the Lord.

Power is thine, O Lord: strength is in thy hand and might is in thine arm.

The Lord is the God of Heaven; the Lord of all the universe is our God.

Sing and rejoice: dance and be glad: show forth the praises of the Ancient One to whom is due all glory and praise.

Let the people of the Name give praise to His glory: to His honor, raise thy voices thou who hast called upon the name of the Lord.

Give praise to the Ancient of Days: to His majesty give praise.

Give glory to the Ancient of Days: to His holiness give worship.

Extol the Ancient of Days: to His name give glory.

Acclaim the Ancient of Days: let His praise be glorious.

Psalm 112

Fire of God burn within me: consume all that is not of thee, O Lord.

Devour the dross of my life, O thou Most Holy: Fire of God burn within me.

Let my life be a sacrifice ready for thy burning.

The wood of my life is laid upon the altar of my repentance: the sacrifice of my humanity is spread upon the wood.

Come Holy Fire, thou Spirit of the Most High: come and fall upon me as thou dist upon the altar on Mount Carmel: as thou didst when Elijah called down thy flames.

Consume me: let all of me be enlivened by the conflagration of thy Spirit, O God.

O Lord, Jesus, Master of my life and God of my soul, Creator of my being and Redeemer of my life, I call upon thee: hear thou me, O God as my voice is lifted before thee.

My heart is thine, O Lord, my heart is thine.

I desire none but thee, Lord Jesus: thou art my deepest desire and the longing of my heart is for more of thee.

Take my life and let it be consecrated, Lord, to thee: Let all within thy servant be thine and thine alone.

Thou art my glory and the lifter of my head: thou hast bought me with the price of Calvary and I am thine, O Lord.

Fire of God, revive me: Fire of God refine me: let my life be pure gold before thee, O Lord: let all dross be consumed by thy Fire, Spirit of God.

Take from me my heart of stone and replace it with thy Presence, O thou Fire of God.

Spirit consume me: burn me up, O God let thy fire refine me and refine me, O God until only Jesus be seen in me.

Fire of God burn within me: incinerate myself and replace it with thy Presence, O Lord.

Let all that is within me shine forth the Lord Jesus: let thy glory shine forth through me that in all thing thou mayest be magnified and the name of Jesus be exalted.

Psalm 113

O Lord, my Lord, how excellent is thy name in all the earth: heaven and earth are filled with thy glory: thy name is exalted by the people of the Blood.

Holy Lord, thou art a majestic and righteous God full of compassion and mercy: thy love hath been displayed at Calvary and thy power shown forth in the empty tomb.

Thou wert born in flesh according to the prophecy of thy Word; thou didst, live and minister and wert crucified, in fulfillment of thy Word; thou didst rise from the dead in glory and majesty and in great power according as thou hadst said.

O how glorious thou art, O Lord; how glorious is thy name and how awesome is thy power.

Thy love brought thee from the realms of heaven to live as a servant; thy love didst take thee to Calvary; thou didst suffer and die for the love that thou didst have for thine own creation.

How great is the love of the Lord? How glorious is His name?

None there be that are like thee, O Lord, and thou wilst share thy glory with no other.

Thou art God alone; in thee, and only in thee, and by faith in thee, is salvation to be found.

Thou art the way, the truth, and the life; No man cometh unto the Father but by thee.

Glorious Lord; Holy Master; Majestic Sovereign and loving God, thou who wast and is and is to come, hallowed be thy name.

Thou, O Lord, art glorious beyond description; thy power is unmeasureable and thy might is displayed in the universe.

O Lord, my Lord, how glorious is thy name in all the earth; thou art a strong and mighty tower; thou art a security to those that follow thee in faith.

Praised be the Lord God of Host and blessed be His name.

Psalm 114

Blow the trumpet in Zion; sound the alarm.

Let the watchman cry forth the coming of the Lord.

Awake ye virgins and light thy lamps for the Bridegroom cometh.

Hear, O ye nations that the time is coming for the heavens to break forth with the power of the Lord and behold, Jesus shall return and reign.

Blow the trumpet in Zion; sound forth the alarm in the holy mountain.

The shall Lord return; let all mankind beware of His coming.

For the Word of the Lord hath said, "Why stand ye here gazing up into heaven? This same Jesus shall likewise come again as he has gone into heaven."

No man knoweth the hour of His coming: neither doth any know the time of His return.

The Lord hath spoken it and His Word is sure: he shall not hold back forever, He shall come even as He said.

The Lord shall cause His glorious voice to be heard: all eyes shall behold the majesty of the returning King.

Rise up ye children of the Lord and bless His name for He has done marvelous things amongst thee: shout forth the praises of the Lord and glorify His name throughout the earth.

Behold, He is the Mighty One: His voice shall be heard through the power of His Word.

He shall come as a thief in the night: no man knoweth the hour of His coming, but His return is sure.

Break forth in dancing ye daughters of the Lord: raise your tambourines and shout unto the Lord thy God.

Raise the trumpets ye saints of the Lord and blow fiercely upon them: sound forth the coming of the Lord.

For the trumpet shall sound and the voice of the archangel shall shout: He shall return in power and glory.

Too long His people have been silent: break forth in a battle cry of might ye Blood-washed throngs and welcome the King of Kings as He returns to claim His throne upon the earth and of His government, and of His kingdom, there shall be no end: give praise unto His name for He alone is worthy.

The Lord our God hath spoken it and, behold, He is a God who cannot lie.

Praise, honor, and glory be unto the Lord Most High: behold the people of Zion shall see Him and acclaim Him to be Lord of all.

Blow the trumpets in Zion: sound the alarm: the Lord Jesus returneth: glory be to His name!

Psalm 115

Thy name, O Lord, is the strength of my life: thou art my surety and truth.

I am called by thy name, O Lord, and I am blessed to be thine.

I will forever give praise unto thy name, O thou Most High for thou hast redeemed me and brought me out of my despair.

In the wastes of my sinfulness I called upon thy name and thou heardest me and lifted me up by thine own power.

There is none like unto thee, O Lord, for thou and thou alone art God.

Even as the heavens declare thy glory and the firmament shows forth thine handiwork, even so shall my soul give praise to thee, O Lord my God for there is none like thee.

Thy name, O Lord, endureth forever: throughout all generations shall thy name be blessed.

While I live will I praise thee, O Lord: whilst breath is within me I shall glorify thy name, O Lord, my God.

I am called by thy name, O Lord God of Hosts: blessed am I to bear the name of Jesus.

Thou art holy forever, O God: may my life be an example of thy holiness.

Strong and mighty is the name of the Lord: by thy name the lame walk and the blinded eyes are opened.

By the name of Jesus Christ of Nazareth shall the broken stand whole and are made well.

There is no other name under heaven, given among men, whereby we must be saved: thy name, Lord Jesus is forever glorious, there is none like thee.

Thou art the Alpha and Omega, the Aleph and Bet, the Beginning and the End: thou art forever and ever God alone.

Thou art the Creator and Sustainer of all things and by thy Word have they been created.

Thy name, O Lord, maketh the demons to tremble and by thy power are they brought low.

Thy name, O Lord, is my strength: thy name hath given me power according to thy Spirit and in thee am I blessed forever.

In all my ways shall I acknowledge the Lord my God and thy name shall continually be blessed by my lips.

The name of the Lord shall forever be a blessing unto all those that call upon thee: to all that call upon thee by faith shalt thou be both Lord and God and thy people shall forever bless thee, O Lord.

Psalm 116

Glorious God, wondrous Sovereign, loving and compassionate Father, I lift my voice to thee for thou art my God and I praise thee.

Thou, O Lord, hast loved be 'ene though my sinfulness doth make me unlovable.

Yet by thy mercy and thy grace thou hast manifested thyself within me by thy Spirit and hath removed my sinful nature by the Blood of Jesus.

O majestic Lord, my soul doth praise thee, my heart doth rejoice in thy salvation.

The power of the Blood doth amaze me: thine ability to forget that which hath been cleansed by the Blood doth astound me.

How glorious thou art, O Lord, how magnificent and splendid thou art, O God.

Humbly I bow before thee, O thou Lord of all, for thou hast freed me from the shackles of mine iniquity and hath given me the freedom of the Holy Ghost, that in thee I may continually rejoice.

Superb and holy Lord, I praise thee: regal Lord of Creation I worship thy name and giveth unto thee mine adoration.

Acclaimed and laudable is the Lord of Hosts: blessed and holy is He.

I came before the Lord dressed in the rags of my sinfulness and my shame and thou hast clothed me regally in the white robes of thine own righteousness, O God.

How can I not praise thee, O Lord? How can my soul, washed in thy Blood, not give thee laud and honor?

Holy art thou, O Lord: glorious and mighty is thy name.

My devotion is thine, O my God; my heart is thy throne, my life is thy throne room.

Receive thou, O my Lord, the worship of thy servant that in thee I might rejoice.

Thou art my God and I praise thee: thou art my Lord, and I give thee glory.

Blessed be the name of the Lord from this time forth and forever.

Psalm 117

O Lord my God, thy servant doth bow before thee and doth bless thy name: for thou art my Savior and my God and in thee only do I trust.

Thou hast redeemed me from destruction and hath raised me to be a joint heir with Christ Jesus: blessed be thy name, O God.

I praise thee, O Lord, for thy power and thy grace: for by thy grace am I saved through faith, and that not of myself, it is thy gift, O God, not of works lest any man should boast.

My soul doth magnify the Lord and in my God do I rejoice.

Thy servant shall forever worship thee, O God, and give praise to thy most holy name, Lord Jesus, my Savior.

Whilst breath is within me, I shall magnify the Lord: for He hath done marvelous things and in Him do I live and have my being.

Thy glory I behold in thy handiwork, O Lord: I behold the mountains arrayed in their autumn splendor and my soul sings, glory be to God, for thy greatness and thy power: there is none like thee, O God.

The majesty of thy name, Lord Jesus doth cause my heart to rejoice and in thee do I forever delight.

Thou hast painted the tapestry of thy glory within thy handiwork, O Lord: thy splendor is seen in thy colors.

The trees of the field shall clap their hands and the mountains shall skip like a roe for the Lord hath decorated the hills in splendor and hath painted His glory in the leaves.

How can my poor tongue speak forth the glory of the Lord in His grandeur? How can thy servant give thee the praises that thy brilliance doth deserve?

Wondrous is the Lord and awesome is His name: His power and glory are seen, His majesty is witnessed in His creation.

Praise the Lord, O my soul: give glory to His majesty and laud to His magnificence.

Thy servant doth bow before thee, O Lord, and in thee shall I ever rest in safety and peace. Glory to the name of the Lord of Host: Praise to the name of Jesus my God.

Psalm 118

Help me, O God, to see through thine eyes. Help me to be able to see with the eyes of compassion and love; the eyes of mercy and grace.

Lift up my soul, O Lord, and give me the ability to see as thou dost see.

My spirit is unable to identify the hurting as thou dost: give me eyes to see like Jesus and a heart of love like unto thine.

Surrounded am I by a world lost and in pain, longing for something without knowing what they doth long for and within me is the answer, the Blood of Jesus can break any yoke and cancel any pain, cover all longing with His Presence.

Lord, thy servant is thine and unto thee shall I ever call in my need for thou alone art God and thou hast brought me into thy Kingdom by thy grace through faith yet so many yet need thee and I am unable, in myself, to help them.

Spirit of the Holy One, transform me. Create in me a clean heart, O God, and renew a right spirit within me that I may show Jesus to those around me.

Enemies compass me about; my heart quakes before their onslaught yet the Lord is with me: He giveth me power when I am powerless and strength in my weakness.

When mine eye is cast upon someone hurting, O God, give me thine eyes to identify that hurt and to reach out with thy Spirit's power to help.

In places where someone is in pain or whose heart is hurting, rise up within me Spirit of God and bring forth thy power through me to heal the hurting and to bring that one to be covered by the Blood that their pain may end by thy power.

Only thy power O God, only thy power can change a heart. Only thy power, O God, only thy power can save a soul.

Thy Blood is ever ready to cleanse a sin-sick soul and make a new creation.

Thy love is ever ready to call a sinner to repentance: if they shall reach out to thee in faith thou art ready to save.

Help me, O God, to be able to see as thou seest. Grant unto thy servant a sensitive heart seeing those lost and hurting, those chained and addicted, those living under attack of the enemy: Help me see as thou dost see and give me the eyes of Jesus and a heart that would reach out in compassion and love by thy Spirit's power.

There is nothing within me that can help another but by thy power, O God: Thy power can rush through me to bring salvation and healing to the nations in Jesus' name.

O Lord, hear my cry. Grant the pleadings of thy servant, O God.

Psalm 119

Aleph*

Praise the Lord ye people of the Lord and give unto God the praises due unto His name.

Bless the Lord and give glory unto His name for the Lord is a God above all gods and a King above all kings.

There is no one like thy God, ye people of the Lord: The King of Heaven is a glorious God, a high and mighty Lord: blessed be His name.

Rejoice and be glad ye people of the Blood: Lift up the name of Jesus and rejoice in the salvation of thy God.

Sing and give praise to the Name, HaShem (the Name), hath raised thee up, yea he hath made thee acceptable in the Beloved.

Jesus is Lord over all the earth and His power shall be seen by all nations. He alone is the Lord of all and His glory is unsearchable.

Bless the name of the Lord: Give praise unto the Lord thy God. Blessed be His name.

Bet

The Blood of Jesus shall never lose its power: It is ever able to cleanse sins and purify hearts:

For the Lord is a God of compassion and a Lord of grace and mercy. His heart is ever ready to hear a prayer of repentance and to forgive all iniquity.

If we confess our sins, He is faithful and just to forgive us our sins and to cleanse us from all unrighteousness. Let His name be praised.

Nothing can wash away sin but the Blood of the Lord: for the blood of bulls and goats was not able to cleanse from sin but the

Blood of Jesus doth eradicate all iniquity when faith doth reach to Him in repentance.

Blessed be the name of the Lord of Host: Jesus Christ is His name.

Gimel

The humble is exalted and the lowly is raised up by the glory of the Risen One: give glory to the Lord.

Those that know not the low are without hope: they are lowered to the pit and shall face the judgment.

But the people who know the Lord shall forever be with Him in glory and shall rule and reign with Him throughout all eternity.

Lift up your hearts to the Lord and give praise to His name because nothing is of worth but Him: His glory is renowned.

Exalt the Lord and bless His name for His mercy and grace: give Him praise for His love and thanks for His compassion.

Seek the Lord while He may be found for time doth run swiftly towards the voice of the Archangel and the trumpet of God: for behold the sands of time run and are gone and none shall recover them.

Daleth

All power belongeth to the Lord of Hosts: Jesus Christ the Righteous is He. He doth sit upon the Heavens and the earth is His footstool.

The mountains quake at His footsteps and the seas roar at the sound of His voice. Lightning flashes in His smile and thunder is His chariot.

The Lord of Glory is high and holy, bow before Him and give Him laud for He hath spoken and the earth was formed, His voice went out and the universe came into being.

Might is in His Word and strength doth flow from His throne unto His people: to those that call upon Him in faith doth His supremacy show forth.

None can stand against Him nor can any be against Him and not be cowed by His majesty and glory: for the Lord of Hosts is the Authority of Righteousness and the Rule of judgment.

He is the great I AM, the self-existent One, the Lord God Almighty and all power is His.

He

Thou art great, O God, and abundant in mercy. Thy grace doth ever uphold my soul for thou hast bought me with a price: the glory of Calvary doth cover me.

The praise of the Lord shall forever be in my mouth: whilst breath is within me I shall forever praise the Lord my God.

Glory and honor art thine, O Lord: dominion and power are thine Most Holy God.

Thou art glorious beyond description, O Lord: forever shall the name of the Lord be praised.

Vau

How wondrous it is to give praise to the Lord: how glorious to expound the majesty of the Holy One.

The name of the Lord is a mighty fortress, the righteous run into it and are safe.

Bless the Lord ye children of the Lord: give praise to His name and lift Him high.

Those that know not the Lord are without hope but the Blood-bought are saved by His grace.

The heathen rejoice in their own prowess: the dependence upon their own ability is the focus of their sinful hearts: But the righteous rejoice in the Lord and in His mercy and grace do they ever delight.

Sing thou daughters of Zion, dance and be glad ye sons of the prophets: for the Lord is thy shield and buckler. None can stand against the majesty of the Lord.

The enemies of the Lord shall fall by the wayside: they shall be trampled in the dust and be remembered no more: but the people of the Lord are a mighty company filled with His Spirit and clothed in His righteousness.

Celebrate the glories of the Lord ye ransomed: bless the name of thy God ye people of the Lord.

Zain

Weeping may last for the night but joy comes in the morning. There is no sorrow in those that know the Lord: they are filled with His glory and shall reign with Him forever.

The joy of the Lord is the strength of the righteous: their power is in the name of their God.

Jesus hath paid the sin-price with His Blood and forever those of faith shall be housed within His kingdom.

Nothing can separate a child of God from His love and benevolence: in the throne room of their God shall they rejoice and give praise.

Cheth

Open the gates of the temple and the King of Glory shall come in. Who is the King of Glory? The Lord strong and mighty, the Lord mighty in battle, He is the King of Glory.

Open the gates of the temple and the King of Glory shall come in. The Lord of Hosts is His name. Give praise unto Him and bless His name.

The children of Israel didst slay the King of Glory. They forsook His righteousness and called for Him to be crucified.

He didst die a criminal's death: He hung upon a cross in shame and agony: yet He didst rise from the dead and behold, He is alive forevermore.

Open the gates of the temple and the King of Glory shall come in. Who is this King of Glory? The Lord Jesus, the Lord Almighty, He is the King of Glory.

Teth

Sing the songs of redemption; the song angels cannot sing: they know not the washing of the Blood nor can they experience grace through faith.

Sing the songs of salvation: what can wash away my sins, nothing but the Blood of Jesus. What can make me whole again; nothing but the Blood of Jesus.

When I survey the wondrous cross on which the Prince of Glory died, my richest gains I count but loss and pour contempt on all my pride.

Rise up ye saints and sing to the Lord: sing the songs of deliverance: the songs of rescue and liberation: the songs of release and emancipation.

Sing and rejoice, rise up and dance, ye saints of the Lord. Lift up thy faith and stand in the power of the Lord.

Sing the songs of salvation: the songs of triumph through the Blood of Jesus.

Sing and rejoice, dance and be glad ye who love the Lord. Make glorious the praises of the Lord ye saints of the Most High.

Jod

The people of the Lord are ready for battle: the Lord God of Hosts is their Captain and in His name shall they assault the enemy.

The saints of God shall rise up with the helmet of salvation upon their heads and the sword of the Spirit (which is the Word of God) in their hands. They shall be girt about with the breastplate of righteousness and with their feet shod with the preparation of the Gospel of peace.

The saints shall arise and conquer in the name of the Lord their God: nothing shall be able to stand against the Church of the Lord Jesus for His name shall be their power and strength.

The enemies of God shall come against the Church but in the name of the Lord shall the Church conquer.

Holding high the Blood-stained banner of the Cross the gates of hell shall not prevail against those who march in faith in Jesus' name.

Caph

I will praise the Lord at all times. His praise shall continually be in my mouth. While there is breath within me I shall ever give glory to the name of Jesus, my Lord and my God.

Unto Him who is able to keep me from falling and to present me faultless before the Presence of His glory with exceeding great joy: to the only wise God my Savior be glory and honor, dominion and power now and forever.

When I step onto the golden streets of glory my voice shall rise in praise to the One who is and who was and who is to come.

My adoration of the Lord my God shall resound throughout the Universe as I lift my voice in praise of the name of Jesus, my God.

Throughout the Milky Way and other galaxies shall my praise echo: Jupiter and Andromeda shall reverberate with the shouts of my adoration of Jesus' name.

The resonance of my praise shall shake the Universe and Haley's comet shall quake in its flight.

The name of the Lord is forever to be praised: His praise shall be made glorious by His servant: yea, this servant of the Lord shall continually lift up His voice in shouts of praise to the Almighty One.

Lamed

The heathen rage: they lift their voice in complaint to God yet do not obey His laws.

The nations rise up against the Lord and His anointed: they defile His name and blaspheme His holiness.

The glories of the Lord they turn to their own: they see but do not acknowledge the sovereignty of the Most High God.

The kingdoms of the earth blaspheme the name of the Lord: they curse and misuse His glorious name.

The Lord will not forever hold back His wrath: his anger is kindled, He shall not forever withhold His justice.

Mem

Seek the Lord while He may be found. Time doth run swiftly: for man is as a breath: as a blade of grass, grown and withered within a day.

His days are fleeting: fast flow the years of man's life; rapidly goes his life.

Spring into summer, summer into fall, fall into winter, so rapid and quick are the days of a man. His life is speedily begun and all too quickly gone for he is as a blink of the eye of the Lord: as a moment in time is the life of a man.

As smoke rising on still air then blown away by a breeze is the time of a man: as a splash upon a rock in a running stream are the days of his life.

Man counts his days as long and tiring, but in reality, the length of his days are as nothing in the playing out of the universe. Man thinks in time but the entirety of his life is as nothing when counted against the glory of the Lord. For with the Lord a day is as a thousand years and a thousand years is as a day. The Lord God is eternal; man in nothing but a snap of fingers, a breath in and out, a drop of rain into an ocean.

Nun

Upon awakening in the morning the praise of the Lord is upon my lips. My heart rises in joy and breaks forth in the adulation of the Lord Jesus my God.

The Lord is good to me at all times. I am blessed by His Presence within me; His Spirit doth make my heart His habitation and by Him I am blessed.

Anoint thy servant, O God, that he may show forth thy blessings to all those that compass round about me.

Pour forth the oil of thine anointing upon me, O Lord: even as the oil didst run upon the head of Aaron even to his beard and his garments, so saturate me, O God, with thy Spirit's anointing. Pour forth thine oil, O Lord. Pour forth thine oil. Anoint me that I may serve thee. Pour forth upon me that I may go forth with thy love and in thy power.

Samech

Thou hast created me to worship, O thou Lord, my God: thou hast cleansed my heart and it is become thy Throne.

Thou hast made me to adore thee, O Lord: thou hast filled me with thy Spirit that I may rejoice and be glad in thee, O thou my Rock and my Salvation.

Whilst I was in my mother's womb thou didst see my future: thou hast laid out the course of my life: though I fought thee and ran from thee, thou didst never leave off loving me and calling me to thyself.

As I have surrendered to thee, O Lord, thou hast made me a vessel of praise: thou hast made me a fountain of exaltation: a well-spring of adoration: a river of glory.

Thou hast made me to worship: thou hast wrought in my heart a reservoir of adoration and I must continually give unto thee the praises due unto thy name O thou Most holy Lord, my Master, my Redeemer, O Jesus thou One True God.

Ain

Jesus shall reign over all the earth: the kings of all nations shall bow before Him: the peoples of all countries shall acknowledge His Lordship and Majesty.

Though now they seek not the Lord neither do they acclaim Him, yet, at the sounding of the shofar, the last trumpet and the voice of the Archangel, the Lord Himself shall descend from heaven with a shout and the dead in Christ shall rise first, then those of us that remain shall be caught up together with them in the clouds to meet the Lord in the air and so shall we ever be with the Lord.

He shall return to the earth, yea, even as He was seen to go up into heaven so shall He come again and place His foot upon the Mount of Olives and all peoples shall see His glory and acknowledge His Kingship.

All nations shall see Him: all the kings of the earth shall bow their knees before the Lord Jesus and proclaim Him Lord of all.

Pe

The power is thine, O Lord: thou hast all authority both in heaven and on earth.

By thy word the wind blows through the tree tops and scours the hill scattering the leaves as it moves.

By the sound of thy voice the seas surge and roar and the waves break themselves against the rocks of the shore.

The mountains quake and the trees clap their hands at thy footsteps.

By thy command the snows fly and the sun scorches the deserts.

By thy word the raven's cry and by thy voice the eagles take to the air in their freedom flight.

Day upon day and night upon night hath been set by thy command, O Lord God of Hosts.

The stars shine at the order of thy Throne: the moon reflects the radiance of the sun by thy charge.

By thy decree, O God, all that is hath been set in order and thou hast said, it was good.

Tzaddi

Exalted, O God, thou art exalted.

Thy name is to be magnified and the glory of thy holiness is to be praised.

Thou and thou alone art the great and mighty God of all creation.

There is none like thee, O Lord; there is none like thee.

All glory and honor is thine, O Ancient of Days: let the praises of thy servant rise as incense laid upon the altar and may it be a sweet savor unto thee, O God.

Let thy servant extol thy majesty, O Lord, and may your Presence be magnified in all the earth.

Blessing and honor, glory and power is thine, O thou Most Holy One: none but thee is due honor, none but thee is worthy of praise.

In all the earth let thy name be exalted: throughout the universe may thy name forever be praised.

Koph

Let my tears come before thee as incense, O God: may thy heart be blessed with my worship and may thou continually be glorified by thy servant.

When I think of thy sacrifice for my salvation, O Lord my God, I am overwhelmed with gratitude and love.

That thou wouldst love a sinner such as I; how wonderful is love like this?

Though my eyes may flow with tears, yet my heart exults in my God. Though I may weep in thy Presence, my tears are thine adoration. I will continually praise thee, O thou my Rock and my salvation. Blessed is thy name, Lord Jesus, my Redeemer.

Resh

Let me see as thou dost see, O God: give me the eyes of Jesus that I may see the needs of people and not their shortcomings.

Let me not see sinfulness or arrogance, neither iniquity nor slothfulness.

Give me the eyes of mercy, the vision of grace, O Lord: let me not take upon myself judgment for judgment is thine, O God and thine alone.

Work in thy servant, O Master, that I may be like unto thee in all things: that my hands wouldst do thy work, my feet go according to thy direction, my heart broken as thine hast been, and my eyes to see as thou seest.

I will ever bless thee, O Lord, for thou art worthy of praise; give to thy servant thine own aspect, O God that in all things I may be like unto thee.

Conform me into the image of Jesus, O Father, that I may be thine own and in being thine, serve thee and thee alone.

Schin

I will praise thee, O Lord, at all times: thy praise shall continually be in my mouth. While I live will I praise thee: while breath doth lie within me I shall utter the praises of the Lord my God.

From the rising of the sun, to the going down of the same, the name of the Lord is to be praised.

When I wake in the morning, I shall bless the Lord of Hosts: at noontime will I give glory to the name of the Lord: when I lay me down to rest, as sleep doth take me, the name of my Lord shall be magnified by thy servant.

I shall forever lift up the name of Jesus for He is worthy and His name is to be glorified.

My heart shall lift up the Lord: my tongue shall speak forth the praises of the Most High. El Elyon, the Lord Most High shall continually be glorified by His servant, and unto His name shall I ever ascribe praise and adoration.

Blessed be the Lord, the Lord God of Hosts, the Holy One, the Ancient of Days.

Tau

Thy Presence, O God is like water in the desert.

Thy Presence is like dew on the parched ground.

When I come before thee, O Lord, and thou dost come and be with me, thy Presence refreshes me and I am complete in thee.

O that I might live in thy Presence, O Most High: that I might dwell in thy courts and worship in thy holy Temple.

O that thy holiness wouldst continually surround me and cover me: that I might be in thy Presence.

My desire shall someday be fulfilled, for by the Blood of Jesus I have been given eternal life, and shall dwell in thy Presence forever.

Blessed be thy name of God. Thy servant doth long to be with thee forever. Amen

* the Aleph, Bet, etc., are twenty-three letters of Hebrew alphabet. Each section of this Psalm is prefaced by one of these letters as in the Biblical Psalm 119

Psalm 120

Glory to God in the highest: Glory was born in Bethlehem, shown on Calvary and was exalted at the empty tomb.

In Him dwelt all of the Godhead bodily and we beheld His glory, the glory as of the only begotten of the Father, full of grace and truth.

Be praised, Lord Jesus, and exalted above all: there is none like unto thy glorious self, O Lord God of Host, Jesus my King.

The praises of the Lord shall continually be in my mouth: all of my days shall be spent in worship of the name of the Holy One, the Lord Jesus.

Whist breath is within me, I shall glorify the name of the Lord: when my eyes close in death, I shall breath my last in honor of the Lord my Master and God.

The wicked misuse thy name, O Lord, and behold not thy glory 'ene though the Universe openly displayed thy majesty.

Honor and glory is thine, O Lord: Majesty and praise be unto thee now and forever.

Let all the saints of the Lord lift up His name in praise: let the Blood-bought shout forth the glory of the Lord Jesus the Christ for He alone is worthy.

Thy name, O Lord, is holy: thou in thyself art Holy. None stand in true holiness but thee, O God: be thou exalted.

Rise up and dance in the Presence of the Holy One ye daughters of the Name: shout and be glad ye brethren for the Lord is thy God and by His Blood hath thou been redeemed.

Sing ye, sisters, praise the Lord in thy songs.

Give glory to the One ye brothers and lift up thy voices to the Risen Lord.

Exceedingly glorious is thy name, O Lord: thou art far beyond all that are called gods.

Thou art enthroned in majesty, O Ancient of Days: thy radiance doth outshine the sun and the rays of thy glory is greater than the universe thou hast created.

Sweep down upon thy people with thy Shekinah, O God: let the cloud of thy Presence settle over those that name thy name.

Blessed and holy art thou, O God: thou art forever exalted and thy name shall be praised throughout eternity. Blessed is the Lord God Almighty.

Psalm 121

Thou hast chosen me, O God, and thy servant doth bow before thy holiness.

Raised from the depths of my sins by the Blood of thy cross, O Lord, I have been chosen as a son of the Father: a joint-heir with the Lord Jesus Christ.

Chosen and blessed I stand in thy glory, O Lord: filled with thy Spirit I am changed from glory into glory as thy power doth flow through me undoing my humanity and replacing it with the image of Jesus.

I was born in iniquity and shapened in sin, yet by thy grace thou hast shed thy love abroad in my heart by the Holy Ghost and hath made me a partaker in the Beloved.

I am blessed beyond measure: chosen in my transgressions, yet thou hath cleansed me: thou hath washed me in thy Blood and though red like crimson, yet now I stand in thy Presence white as snow.

Thou hast not held mine iniquity against me neither hath thou cast me off because of my sins: but in my unrighteousness thou didst raise me and cleanse me, filled me with thy Spirit and made me thy son.

How could I measure thy grace, O God: or how could I gauge thy mercy?

How could I assess thy affection for me, O Most High: or how could I appraise thy great love, O Ancient of Days?

There is no measure of thy love, O God: there is no measuring of thy mercy and grace: for the love of God is abundant and free, flowing from thy heart. Thy love didst bring thee from the portals of Glory into the form of a man and lead thee to Calvary where thou didst willingly lay down thy life that I might be washed in thy Blood and conformed into thy righteousness, clothed in the white robes of thy holiness.

Thou hast chosen me, O God, and my heart is thy Throne: my life is thine, O God, for thou hast purchased me with thy Blood and I am made to stand in thy holiness and thy righteousness.

Thou hast chosen me, as unworthy as I am and thou hast made me a new creation is Christ Jesus.

Thy servant doth bow before thee, O Holy One and doth praise thee for who thou art.

Thou and thou alone art a God of love and mercy, O Lord: grace doth flow from thy Throne and by thy grace I am saved through faith, and that not of myself it is thy gift, O God, not of works lest any man shouldst boast.

O Lord, how I praise thee. O God, how I magnify thee.

Thy love is a balm to me O God: a salve for my soul.

Thou hast chosen me, O Lord, and I lift up thy name in praise and honor: for thou art my God and I worship thee alone. Thou art my God and the lifter of my head.

Honor and glory is thine, O God: thou art highly exalted and thy servant shall forever give thanks unto thee for thy goodness and thy love, which hath made me thy child and as a son I stand before thee to magnify thy name forever.

Psalm 122

O thou that rulest the universe, thou God of my heart, hear me.

My heart is sore within me. The ghosts of past hurts hover over me and shriek their remembrances into my ears.

Come to me, O thou Comforter; come and silence the ghosts of past hurts: Let not their remembrances taint my joy in thee.

Thou art the strength of my life, O Lord: thou hast given unto me eternal life through Jesus Christ my Lord and I am thine, body, heart, mind and soul.

My life is thine because of thy great grace and thy eternal love. Thy love didst bring thee to earth as a babe and thou didst grow into my Savior and the Savior of mankind.

In my life, O Lord, there hast been times of deep hurt: memories that even after many years still hurt when brought to mind. Place the salve of thy comfort upon me, O God.

Thou Spirit of Holiness who art my true and constant Comforter, come to me, I pray.

Tear down the walls of memorious hurt that haunt me. Renew within me, O God, the joys of thy salvation and bring to me once again the fullness of thy peace.

The past is as melted snow under a strong sun: they are as grass that is grown, withers, dies, and blows away.

Memories of life are the signposts that are marked along the pathways of mine existence: they show the places I have been and stand as memorials that have made me into who I am now.

But thou, O Lord, hath changed my pathways: thou hast brought about a new life within me by thy Spirit's Presence and I am a new creation in Christ Jesus, my Lord.

Let not the past bring pain, O God. Allow the past to blow away in the winds of thy mercy: let them be memories without pain, occurrences without hurt, and recollections without torment.

Thou, O Lord, hath changed my heart from a heart of sinful stone into a heart melted by thy grace and consumed by thy Spirit's infilling: bring to my memories the same grace as thou didst use on my sins and cleanse me of all pain and anguish, sorrow and grief and let me see them as markers along the journey of my life but without any power to bring hurt.

Thy grace, O Lord, is my sustenance and sure fortification. Thy Spirit brings me life and joy, strength and peace and I am content in thee. My heart rejoices in thee, O my God, and I am blessed in thee forever.

Psalm 123

Consume me, O God, with thy Presence; stretch forth the covering of thy Shekinah and wrap thy glory around me, O thou Most High.

Take thy servant as a sacrifice, O Lord; my life is laid on the altar before thee, O God; accept thou me.

Envelop me in thy Presence, O Lord; shield me with thy glory and let thy servant behold the wonders of thy majesty in all thy Spirit's power.

Thou art my shelter, O Lord, my sure and certain defense through all the troubles of life.

By thy power I am strong; by thy glory I am more than a conqueror through Jesus Christ my Lord.

I have no desire but thee, O my God; thou art my strong Deliverer and the uplifter of my head.

As thou didst cover Israel with the Cloud of thy Presence, O Lord, cover thou me; wrap me in the white robes of thy righteousness that I may stand unblemished before thee and as thou dost regard me thou shalt see only the Blood of Jesus and His likeness within me by thine own power, O God.

Clothe me with thy splendor, O God that I may be like thee; let the image of Jesus be seen in me, O thou Most Holy.

Shine upon me with the Light of thy Countenance that I may reflect thy ways to the world and thy majesty to those blinded to thy truth.

Spring up in me, O God as a wellspring in the desert; as water from the Rock, rise up and flow through me, O Lord.

Thou art the Living Water of hope and regeneration: thou givest life by the streams of thy Presence.

Wash over me, O God: wash and cover me: cleanse and fill me: restore and renew me, O thou Fountain of power and glory.

Consume me, O God with thy Presence: let me live only and fully for thee and thee alone.

Let all mine iniquity be cleansed by thy Blood, Lord Jesus: let Calvary's crimson flow wash away all traces and taint of unrighteousness in me and let me stand clothed in thy glory and thy Presence.

Let the cloud of thy Radiance cover me as a garment, O Most High. Wrap me in thy holiness that I may be holy before thee.

Let all my life before thee, O God, be as holiness unto the Lord.

Psalm 124

When I consider the works of thy hands, O God, I am amazed at thy proliferation: thy glory shines forth in thy creation, O Most High.

I look and behold the mountains covered in new snow, glistening in the sunshine and sparkling like diamonds and my heart whelms up in praise.

I breath deeply of the pine scented air and my soul rises in exaltation of thy majesty, O Lord.

As I watch and behold the squirrels playing in the branches of a tree, or see a rabbit scurrying alone a path or see a fawn standing in the distance, my heart worships the One who spoke it all into existence and I praise thee, O God.

Thou art mighty and glorious, O Lord: there is none like unto thee, O Most Holy: no one has the power that thou dost possess, O God.

I walk by a stream and the water rushing over the rocks sings praise unto their Creator: the beauty around me reflects the splendor of the Lord of Hosts.

Even a dead tree standing alongside of the brook shows its own silent, aged grandeur. Only the mind of the Lord could bring forth such diverse and intricate luxury and finery within the Creation of His Words.

Glory is thine, O Lord: the praises of my heart belong only to thee, for thou and thou alone, art the Great and Matchless God of the Universe, the Author of all Existence.

I will lift up my hands in praise unto thee, O God: my heart swells within me as I worship the name of the Lord my God.

How can I give thee enough praise, O Lord? How can my poor tongue be able to speak forth the glory that thou art worthy of, O Most High.

I bow my heart before thee, O Ancient of Days: my soul doth bless the Lord for His mercy and grace, His love and His comfort, His care, and His peace.

O magnify the Lord with me and let us praise the name of the Lord forever.

Thou art holy, O Lord, and glorious in all thy ways: I am humbled before thee, O God, and I worship thee for who thou art.

My heart doth praise the Lord my God and my soul worships His majesty.

Praise and honor, glory and power is thine, O God, and thy servant doth bow in meekness before the awesomeness of thy Presence, O Most High. Blessed be the Lord God of Hosts now and forevermore. Glory to His name.

Psalm 125

Come Lord Jesus: come and take thy people home.

My heart doth long for the Presence of the Lord my God: my soul longs for the courts of the Lord.

Thou hast promised, Lord Jesus, that thou wouldst come again even as thou didst go into heaven.

Thy Word doth testify that the Lord Himself shall descend from heaven with a shout, with the voice of the Archangel and the trump of God, and the dead in Christ shall rise first, then those of us that remain shall be caught up together with them in the air, and so shall we ever be with the Lord.

Thy servant doth long to be with thee, O Lord: to bow at thy feet and worship thee face-to-face is the dearest desire of my heart.

I do not long for pearly gates or golden street, O Most High, but to see the face of Jesus, to behold thy blessed hands and feet which were wounded for me: to behold Him which I love most dearly but whom I have never yet seen face to face.

O Lord Jesus, I long to be with thee: the cares of this world oft times overwhelm me and my soul is repulsed by the sin and iniquity that doth continually surrounding me: I long for the Presence of thy holiness: my soul yearns to worship in the Tabernacle of thy Glory, to bow my knees before thee and declare my allegiance to thee, O Lord.

My soul doth crave the courtyards of my God: to be with thee, and to behold thee is the entreaty of my heart.

Father, only thou knowest the time that Jesus will return, but my heart doth cry, Come Lord Jesus.

Even in my longing for thee, O my God, I have to pray, hold back, O Lord. Do not yet let the Archangel shout, nor the trumpet sound.

Too many souls yet need to know thee, Lord Jesus. Too many have not given their hearts to thee and been born again.

Thousands remain without the Gospel, yet, O Lord: too many yet need to know thee and hear thy Word.

Although thy Word has been spread to all continents and peoples, yet there remain too many that are bound by their iniquity and the chains of addictions and perversions. They need thee, O Lord. They need the cleansing of thy Blood and the new birth that only thou canst provide.

My heart doth long to be with thee, O God, yet it is better that I remain that thy Word might still be declared to those that know thee not.

Thy servant doth long for thy Presence and for the glory of thy Face, O Jesus, my Lord. Thy servant doth long to be with thee forever. Nothing is as dear to my heart then to be with thee, O Lord, to kneel before thee and spend the first ten thousand years giving thanks unto thee for thy sacrifice for me and for thy Blood.

Yet, Lord Jesus, 'ene as I long to be with thee, my heart cries for more souls, O my God: More souls for thy kingdom and for thy glory.

Not for my advancement, O Lord, not for my good but for thee and thee alone: for thy glory and thy honor and that thou mayest have many more in thy Presence, when the trump doth sound, that will praise thee for thy mercy, thy grace and thy Blood.

Let thy servant carry the Blood-stained banner of thy kingdom to those that know thee not: let thy servant advance thy kingdom, O my God, through thy power and might by thy Most Holy Spirit which doth dwell within me.

Let thy name be praised and thy kingdom advanced: though I long to be with thee, Lord Jesus, I cannot ask thee to come yet.

My heart is torn betwixt my desire to see thy face and my longing for souls added to thy kingdom, O God.

Pour forth thy Spirit, O Lord, upon all flesh that all may know thee, bow before thee and declare that thou art Lord of all.

Come, Lord Jesus, and saturate thy servant with thy powerful Spirit that thy Word might be declared through thy might and that souls be added to thy kingdom and thy Name declared as holy.

Come, Lord Jesus, come and empower thy servant.

Psalm 126

The Lord of Hosts is the Sovereign of the Universe: make His praise glorious.

The Lord has compassion on the poor and upholds the weary: make His praise glorious.

The Lord shows grace to those in need and mercy to those that call upon Him: make His praise glorious.

The Lord hath provided salvation to all those that come to Him in faith: make His praise glorious.

The Lord shall provide protection and comfort for His people: make His praise glorious.

Peace and prosperity are the benefits of the people of the Lord: make His praise glorious.

The Lord is watchful over His people; His eyes are ever upon the people of His name: make His praise glorious.

The Lord shall provide a fortress of His power for those that are His: make His praise glorious.

The Spirit of the Lord shall provide clothes of righteousness to those that are Blood washed: make His praise glorious.

White robes shall be the garments of the His people: make His praise glorious.

The Lord brings from the dust those that call upon Him: make His praise glorious.

Those that call upon Him in truth shall he raise up: make His praise glorious.

The song of the redeemed shall be the battle hymn of those that have been washed in the Blood of the Lamb: make His praise glorious.

Songs of grace through Calvary shall be the anthem of the Blood-bought: make His praise glorious.

Eternal life shall be unto those that call upon the Lord in faith and give their hearts to the Lord: make His praise glorious.

Heaven awaits all those that have come to the Father through Christ Jesus the Lord: make His praise glorious.

Golden streets shall be the walkways of the redeemed: make His praise glorious.

Mansions of glory are being prepared for all the people of the Name: make His praise glorious.

The Lord is faithful and just: make His praise glorious.

The Lord is truth and righteousness: make His praise glorious.

The Lord is the way, the truth, and the life: make His praise glorious.

No man cometh unto the Father but through the Lord Jesus: make His praise glorious.

The Lord shall come again: make His praise glorious.

Jesus shall return to take up His people: make His praise glorious.

And so shall we ever be with the Lord: make His praise glorious.

Psalm 127

Great Lord of All, thy name is glorious: thou art wondrous to think upon and awesome in all thy aspects.

Hear the voice of thy servant, O Lord, as it is raised in praise unto thy majesty: to the glory of thy name do I lift up my voice, O Lord my God.

Thou art worthy, O Lord of all praise and adoration: worship and reverence, exaltation and honor is due unto thee, O Most High.

There is none like unto the Ancient of Days, the Lord Most High, the High and Holy One: there is none like thee, O God.

The adulation of thy servant is only unto thee, O Lord, for thou art my God and thee only do I worship.

My knees shall bow to none but the Lord of Hosts: to no other than the Lord Christ shall I bow in homage and devotion.

I shall forever lift mine eyes to Calvary in thanksgiving and praise for what thou hast done for me, O Lord.

My poor voice can never give thee praise enough to match thy glory: were I to have a thousand tongues, I yet could not speak forth enough of thy praise.

When I wake in the morning my heart doth sing, I worship thee because of who thou art: when I lay be down to sleep at night my last thoughts are, blessed be the Lord God Almighty, who was, and is, and is to come.

My heart doth dwell on the Lord my God: on the majesty of the Lord Christ shall my heart forever dwell.

Thou doth rule my life, Lord Jesus, and unto thee shall I forever raise my exaltations.

Day by day thy servant doth praise thee, O God, and unto thy name alone do I give reverence.

Thou hast bought me with a price, O Lord: the wondrous price of thine own Blood didst thou pay for my life.

Calvary covers it all: none of mine iniquity doth thou remember, O God because of the washing of thine own Blood.

The praises of the Lord my God shall forever be a banner flying ore the fortress of my salvation.

The holiness of my God doth clothe me as a garment, and I stand righteous before thee because of thine own Presence.

Thou hast made me thy habitation, O God, and I stand sanctified in thee.

Thy Spirit hath made thy dwelling within me and I am thy tabernacle, O Lord my God, my Savior and my King.

The Lord is great and mighty is His name: the worship of the Lord shall forever be my dwelling place and I shall live within thy holy habitation forever.

My heart is thy throne room, O Lord: my soul is thy Temple.

There is no building of stone or mortar that could be the dwelling place of the Most High: yet in the hearts of those that thou hast washed in thy Blood and sanctified by thy Spirit shall thou forever reside.

Thou art wondrous, O God, and altogether holy art thou.

Forever shall I praise the Lord my God: while in my flesh I shall glorify the Lord and when taken to my heavenly Home I shall throughout eternity give praise to He is who is the Lord of my heart and of all creation.

Blessed is the name of the Lord Jesus Christ and glorious is His praise raised up by His servant.

Psalm 128

O how the wicked rage against the things of the Lord: they cry out that there is no God and in their ignorance they deny His authority and power.

The signs of the glory of the Lord are all around: creation speaks the majesty of the Lord.

Look to the mountains and behold His handiwork: behold the sky at night and see His deeds.

Consider a rose or look upon a violet: the lilies of the valley testify to the artistry of the Lord.

He spoke, His Word went forth, and all that exists came into being:

The wicked say not so: they deny God's being and His power.

But the Lord reigns over all the universe: His majesty is unending and of His power there is no equal.

Behold, those that deny the Lord are as a dog growling over a bone where no one tries to take it from him: they raise their growls and gnaw away at a dead thing. This is the plight of the wicked.

But the children of the Lord rejoice in His power: they sing songs to the glory of the Lord and the majesty of His name.

The Lord is high and holy and His people bless His name.

The righteous walk into the mountains and give praise to the Lord for His handiwork: they walk into a field and are filled with wonder at the innovation, production, and artistry of the Word of the Lord.

Praises rise from the hearts of God's people: they rejoice in His love and are grateful for His mercy and grace.

The daughters of the Lord dance in His Presence: the men lift holy hands unto His glory.

Peace reigns in the hearts of the holy: the righteous have the Lord their God as their fortress.

The Spirit of the Lord upholds the Blood-bought: His power changes lives for His glory.

Those who deny the Lord are wicked and undone, saturated in their own iniquity and dead in their trespasses and sins.

They blaspheme the name of the Lord and call their sins as choices: they trust in their own resources and compound their sins.

But the children of the Lord are seen as sinless by the Lord because of the Blood of the Lamb: the Lord Christ hath given Himself as sacrifice that whosoever believeth in Him shall not perish but have everlasting life.

Thus do the righteous delight in the Lord for He hath given them eternal life through Jesus Christ the Lord.

Rage on ye wicked and rant ye iniquitous for thy raging is vain and thy ranting is useless for the Lord God reigns and of His Kingdom there shall be no end.

The Lord clothes His people in His righteousness and covers them with His power as with a garment.

The holiness of the Lord surrounds those that are His and He spreads forth His power to encompass them.

Nothing shall be able to separate us from the love of God that is in Christ Jesus our Lord.

All see the handiwork of the Lord: eyes have they but they do not comprehend: ears have they but they witness not unto the truth. They consult only their own conceit and do not understand what the Lord hath wrought for them.

The Lord shall reign forever: His kingdom shall not end: His power shall nere bc diminished.

Open thine eyes ye wicked: open thy hearts that the Lord may do a new thing in thee. Break open the closet of thy conceit and behold the wonders of the Lord that surround thee.

Psalm 129

I love to tell the story of unseen things above; of Jesus and His glory, of Jesus and His love.

I love to tell the story because I know 'tis true. It satisfies my longing like nothing else can do.

I love to tell the story. 'Twill be my theme in glory: To tell the old, old story of Jesus and His love.

Thy name, O Lord, is glorious to my soul: thou doth bless me continually by the power of thy name.

Thou hast bought and cleansed me and hath given me eternal life and my soul doth rejoice in thee.

I will sing the wondrous story of the Christ Who died for me. How He left His home in glory for the cross of Calvary. Yes, I'll sing the wondrous story of the Christ who died for me, Sing it with the saints in glory, gathered by the crystal sea.

Thy song, O Lord, doth rise within me to praise thy wondrous name: I shall forever sing of thy glory and all that thou hast done for me.

Nothing shall still within me the song of thy salvation, O my Lord Christ: whilst I have breath I shall lift my voice unto thee, O Lord, and praise thy holy name.

Thy name is power, O Lord: wrapped within thy name is all the power of thy Godhead.

No greater power exists than the name of the Lord Jesus Christ. He and He alone is the omnipotent One, the God of all Creation, the Lord of Life, the Ancient of Days, the Holy One.

Jesus, Jesus, Jesus, sweetest name I know; Fills my every longing; keeps me singing as I go.

The name of the Lord is a strong and mighty tower. Thy name is a shelter like no other. Thy name, let the nations sing it louder, nothing has the power to save, like thy name.

Oh how my heart bubbles up with the praises of thy name, O Lord. My mind goes back and my heart brings forth the songs of the redeemed and by them thy name is glorified.

I sing of thy power, thy love, and thy grace but my deepest love is to sing of the name of my Lord and Savior, Jesus the Christ.

There is a name I love to hear, I love to sing its worth; It sounds like music in mine ear, The sweetest name on earth.

It tells me of a Savior's love, who died to set me free; It tells me of His precious blood, The sinner's perfect plea.

It tells of One whose loving heart can feel my deepest woe, who in each sorrow bears a part that none can bear below.

Oh how I love Jesus: thou art my God yet thou art also my dearest friend.

Thou art my King yet thou art my constant companion.

Nothing shall keep thy servant from singing the praises of thy name, O Lord.

Jesus, forever shall I glorify thy name: I will sing of thy love until my dying day, then yet in Heaven with thee, I shall throughout eternity sing the wonders of thy name.

Psalm 130

Thou doth amaze me, O God: how thou dost work is continually astonishing.

Thou truly art Jehovah-jireh, the Lord that provides.

Thou makest a way where there seemeth to be no way: thou makest roadways in the desert and pathways in the barren places.

Thy hand doth make provision 'ene in times of emptiness and depravity.

Thou doth see where I have need and by thy provision thou dost astound me.

How thou dost work staggers mine imagination: thou art marvelous in how thou dost provide.

My soul doth rejoice before thee for thou dost make provision in times when I have not made petitioned unto thee.

Jehovah-jireh, thou art glorious in all thy aspects yet thy supply in time of need doth impart untold blessings unto my soul.

Thou hast granted unto thy servant the gifts of thy hand and humbly I bow before thee and thank thee for thy goodness to me.

Thou hast made me accepted in the Beloved and I am thy servant in truth: yet thou hast opened thy hand of grace and hath provided for me in my time of need.

I didst not call upon thee, nor did I petition thy Throne for my need: yet thou, in thy great knowledge hath taken care of my needs by thy all-knowing greatness.

Water thou didst make in the desert: quail and manna didst thou provide for thy people.

The brazen serpent was lifted up according to thy voice and thy people didst receive healing as they gazed upon it.

Thou didst keep clothing and shoes from wearing out as thy people didst journey through the desert.

Thy hand kept thy people supplied and in thy provision didst they complete their journey.

Thou art a God of supply: all that thy servant doth need thou doth bestow upon him.

O Lord, my God, I am humbled by thy hand: by the impartation of thy grace doth I bow before thee.

Thanks be to God for His loving-kindness and His tender mercies: for His care and provision do I raise up my voice in thanksgiving.

Gratefully do I acknowledge the working of the hand of my God: for the provision of my unspoken need do I praise the Lord my God.

Thou seest my life and thou hath all things in thy control: thou doth make a way.

O great Waymaker, thy servant doth praise thy name: with a grateful heart do I bow before thee and call thee blessed.

Glorious and astounding is the Lord Jehovah-jireh: wondrous and great is the working of His hands.

Let all the saints of the Lord arise and give praise to the wondrousness of the Lord their God.

Thy servant doth praise thee, O God, and with a grateful heart doth he make his praises known unto thee.

Blessed is the Lord God of Hosts and blessed is His name forevermore.

Psalm 131

The enemy hath been defeated by the power of the Blood: Jesus was raised from the dead unto total victory.

The Blood of the Lord Jesus cleanses from all sin: eradication of iniquity is within the Blood of the Lord.

The prince of the powers of the air, the enemy of all souls hath found defeat at Calvary.

The empty grave testifies to the power and excellence of the Lord Jesus Christ.

This same Spirit that raised Christ from the dead so also likewise quicken your mortal bodies by His Spirit that dwelleth in thee.

No demon or spirit, principality or power can stand against the authority of the Blood of Jesus.

The devil is a liar and the father of lies. There is no truth within him. He is from the beginning a liar who doth roam the earth seeking those that he may devour.

He thinks himself to be something when he is nothing: the Blood of Jesus hath brought him low: his power and authority ended when the Blood flowed and the tomb became empty.

Risen and victorious is the Lord Christ: victorious is He over death, hell and the grave.

Enemy of my soul, the Blood of Jesus is against thee: thou canst not stand against the power of the Blood.

Christ hath made sacrifice once for all that whosoever believeth in Him shall not perish but have everlasting life.

The sacrifice of the Lord Christ hath brought unto the faithful, everlasting life according to the power of the Blood.

Thou art defeated, O enemy: naught that thou canst do can save thee from the eternal fires and torments of hell: for thou art in rebellion against God and thou hast been overcome by the

Blood of the Lamb: thou hast been overpowered by the Blood of Jesus: thou art conquered by Calvary's crimson flow.

Thou art vanquished, ye devils: thou art crushed by the power of the Risen One: thine authority hath been routed and thou art subjugated unto the Lord Christ.

Nothing can stand against the victorious power of the Blood.

Thanks be unto thee, Lord Jesus, for that which doth wash away all sin and doth turn my crimson iniquities into white robes of thine own righteousness.

Not of works of righteousness which I have done but by His mercy hath He shed His Blood that all who come to Him in faith, believing, shall have eternal life through Jesus Christ the Lord.

Psalm 132

Praise be unto thee, O Lord my God: praise be to thee.

Thou surroundeth me with thy Presence and in thee I am safe.

Thou doth compass me about with thy grace and thy Spirit doth dwell within me. Praised be thy name.

Give ear unto me ye people of the Lord: harken to my voice all ye saints.

The Lord is great in power and majestic in His glory: this grace doth cover all who call upon Him in faith.

The Blood of the Lord Christ taketh away all sins: inquity is vanquished by the Blood of the Lord.

My soul doth praise thee, O Lord, for thy greatness and thy power: for thy mercy shown towards me at Calvary do I give praise unto thee.

Be Thou my Vision, O Lord of my heart; Naught be all else to me, save that Thou art. Thou my best thought, by day or by night, waking or sleeping, Thy Presence my light.

Consume thou me, O God, that, in thee, I may become thy sure and true servant.

Consume all my life, my heart, and my soul: Spirit of God make thou me whole.

The brightness of the Lord is the light of my life: thou doth give light unto my way by thy Word, O God: thy Word is a lamp unto my feet and a light unto my path.

Grant me understanding, O Lord: let the light of thy Spirit bring illumination to my heart by thy Word.

Thou hast brought me from the depths, O God and hath set me within the Beloved by thy love and thy grace.

Lord, Jesus, forever shall my heart rejoice in thee: nothing shall quell the praises that shall spring forth from my soul.

High King of Heaven, my victory won, may I reach heaven's joys, O bright Heaven's sun! Heart of my own heart, whatever befall, still be my vision, O Ruler of all.

Thou dost sit in majesty, O Lord my God: the universe is thy throne room and the earth is thy footstool.

Thou art King of all: blessed is thy name.

Thou art Lord of life: praise be unto thee.

Thou art a sure and safe refuge for all those that call upon the name of the Lord: to all those that call upon thee in faith, thou art forever faithful.

Thou art Judge of all creation: by thy great wisdom shall the earth be judged.

Great is Thy faithfulness, O God my Father: There is no shadow of turning with Thee; Thou changest not, Thy compassions, they fail not: As Thou hast been Thou forever wilt be.

Thy faithfulness doth support thy saints, O God: by thy loving-kindness are they upheld.

Praise and honor, glory and power art thine forever, O Lord: thy name, Lord Jesus is forever to be exalted.

Throughout eternity my voice shall give glory to the Lord my God: unto Jesus my Lord shall I forever give praise.

O ye saints of the Lord, give praise to His name: to the name of the Lord give glory and honor.

Strike up the harps and bring forth the tambourines: bring forth music and dancing that the name of the Lord may be praised.

Sound the trumpets and blow the ram's horns: play upon the organs and ring forth the cymbals in honor of the glory of the Lord of Hosts.

To the Captain of the Armies of the Lord give forth praise: to all of His greatness break forth in rejoicing.

Praise be unto thee, O Lord my God: praise be unto thee.

Psalm 133

Unworthy! I am so unworthy: there is nothing within me that is deserving of thy grace, O God.

My sins are ever before mine eyes: my iniquities are within my remembrance.

In sin was I conceived and in iniquity was I born: my nature is corrupt and immoral.

Yet in love thou didst come to dwell on this earth, O Lord, to provide full salvation through thy Blood: the sacrifice of Jesus purchased for me not only salvation and eternal life but freedom from my unworthiness and all my iniquity.

A new creation in Christ Jesus am I because of His precious Blood.

Thou hast declared me to be clothed with thine own righteousness, O Lord, and before thee do I stand clothed in white robes.

Thou art my righteousness, O Lord, and in thee am I free of all sin and transgression.

Alone I am unworthy yet in Christ Jesus I am a child of the Father and a joint heir with Christ Jesus my Lord.

My sins have been banished and cast as far as the east is from the west.

Because of the Lord Christ thou rememberest not mine iniquity and in thee am I made new because of thy grace.

Love found me, grace redeemed me, and mercy gave me eternal life through Jesus Christ my Lord.

There is naught within me that is deserving of the grace of the Lord: yet grace covers me as I reach unto thee with faith, O God.

Thou bringest me to glory by thy love for me: thou crownest me with lovingkindness and they tender mercies.

Thou hast made me accepted in the Beloved and by Christ Jesus I am made more than a conqueror.

There is no condemnation to those that are in Christ Jesus: to those that walk not after the flesh but after the Spirit.

Thou hath made me thy habitation, O God, by thy Spirit and I am filled with thy glory and thy righteousness because of thee.

Thou hast covered me with thy Blood: thou hast taken my crimson, sin-sick soul and hath washed me white as snow by thy Blood.

I have been reconciled to my God because of the Blood of Jesus: because of thy life's Blood, O Lord, I am brought nigh unto thee.

Forever shall I give praise unto thee, O Lord my God, for thou hast washed me in the Blood and thou hast given me a heart of flesh where once was a heart of stone.

Thou hast changed me into a new creation by thy washing, O God, and forever shall I bless thy name.

Glory and honor are thine, O Lord, and all my praises shall forever rise to thee.

Blessed be the name of the Lord Jesus the Christ, Sovereign Lord of all creation and Lord of my life.

Dominion and power are thine, O Lord, and the joy of my life comes from thee: for thou and thou alone art my happiness and my delight: Blessed be thy name forevermore.

Psalm 134

Thy Presence, O God, art the joy of my life: surrounded by thy glory my soul doth exalt in thee.

Thy servant doth continually rejoice in thee: thy praises rise from my soul and my heart giveth adoration to thy name.

I stand in thy Presence as a cool stream bursting forth from a hidden place in the desert: as a wellspring art thou to my parched soul.

When I stand in thy anointing, O God, I am filled with thy purity and thy holiness.

Filled with thy Presence I am able to run through a troop and jump over a wall: no stronghold couldst stand against me as I am filled with thee and thy glorious Presence.

The anointing of the Lord is like unto me as the oil that flowed from the beard, even Aaron's beard as thou didst cover him with thy Presence and claimed him as thy High Priest.

As dew in the morning, or the sparkling of sunshine on new snow art thou to me, O God.

Thou art my glory and my rejoicing, O Lord of Hosts: my sufficiency and support art thou.

Thou liftest me up in sorrow and shineth upon me in dark times: the Lord lights up the shadows of life and gives radiance to gloom.

When thou comest to me, O God, and thou dost wrap thine arms around me; my soul is refreshed and in thee am I revived.

Thou dost rejuvenate me as with cool water: even as a fountain to my thirst art thou, O Lord.

Thy glory is my rejoicing: thy Presence my delight.

Thou art always to me a triumph, O God, and my jubilation.

The Lord Christ is my joy and my delight: in the Lord Jesus my God am I in elation and wonder.

When I seek thee, thou art there: when I call upon thee, thou dost come unto me and doth enfold me in thine arms.

When my tears flow as praise unto thee thou dost encircle me with thy Presence and in thee am I covered as with a mantle, even as Elijah's mantle.

Thou dost clothe me in thy righteousness and doth cover me as with a garment.

Thy Presence, O Lord, doth thrill my soul: thy glory, Lord Jesus, doth stir my heart to rejoicing.

As a starving man presented with a banquet am I in thee, O God: my soul is satisfied and my heart is made full.

As a dying vine in the wilderness, or a parched plant am I without thee, O God.

My soul is dry and arid, O Lord, without thy Presence: apart from my Lord Jesus I am desiccated and my soul doth gasp for the living water of thy Spirit.

Yet when I stand in thy Presence, O Lord, I am washed with refreshing and bathed in the sweet water of thy glory.

Thou doth make me rejoice, Lord, Jesus, and in thee am I filled with satisfaction: nothing doth bring joy to my heart as thy Presence, O Lord my God.

Thou doth stretch forth thy nail-scarred hands to me and I am enfolded within thy Spirit and in thee I am made whole.

Thy Presence, O Lord, art the thrill of my life and the delight of my soul: thy servant doth bask in thy glory.

O that I might dwell in the Presence of the Lord forever and in thy Being might I make mine habitation.

Psalm 135

The Lord is gracious and slow to anger; full of mercy and of great love.

The Lord remembers not the sins of those that have been washed in the Blood: by the Blood of Jesus doth the Lord remember not our sins.

The Lord is a God above all gods: His power is immutable and His glory is unsearchable.

The Lord reigns in heaven: His throne room is eternal.

By His Word didst He make all that exists: His word went forth and the universe came into existence.

Yet the Lord dwelleth not in the universe. The universe doth exist within the Lord our God: for in Him do we live and move and have our being.

The Lord is awesome in power and great in might.

The Lord is above all things and by His power are all things sustained.

Rise up ye saints and exalt the Lord thy God: give unto His name high praises.

To the High King of Heaven give thou great adoration and praise: let His praises resound throughout all places.

Bless the Lord who made the heavens and the earth: bless His name and give glory unto His most glorious power.

The angels do continually give praise to His power: Holy, holy, holy is the Lord God Almighty.

Let the saints of the Lord begin now to uphold the name of their God and to His majesty give praise.

The Lord is high and holy; His name is above all names.

The Lord is a God of mercy: His judgments are sure and right.

The great God of All cannot lie: neither can deceit or falsehood be found in Him.

The Lord is righteous in all His being: all His aspects are righteous and holy.

Who can stand in the Presence of the Lord God of Hosts: who can stand before His holiness and live?

The Lord hath a strong arm and a powerful right hand: no army can withstand the power of the Lord: no dominion or stronghold can withstand the might of the Lord.

Rise up and shout, ye Blood-washed saints: rise up and cry forth the glory of the Lord.

Hold not thy tongues ye saints of the Lord: hold not thy peace but give praise to the name of thy God.

The Lord is a blessing to His saints and a terror to His enemies: to those that stand against the Lord, He shall rise up in righteous judgment and they shall be no more.

Those that oppose the Lord shall be as dust blown away with the wind: there shall be no remembrance of them.

As dry leaves crushed under foot shall the foes of the Lord be: they shall dry up and be trodden down.

The Lord hath the universe as His throne room and the earth is His footstool: He reigns in power and glory, may His name be glorified.

The Lord upholds His people and sustains them by His promises: the promises of the Lord are sure and amen.

Nothing can stand against the power of the Lord: against His power can no one withstand.

The Lord is awesome in majesty and glorious in all His aspects: in all His ways He is strong and able to do exceedingly, abundantly above anything that any could ask or think.

The Lord is great and greatly to be praised: the name of the Lord is to be exalted above all: He alone is God!

Psalm 136

Let the Blood-bought arise: arise ye Blood-bought Saints and lift up the banner of the Lord Jesus thy King.

Bring forth the praises of the One who was and is and is to come: the Lord Christ is poised in Heaven awaiting the sounding of the trumpet.

Shout all ye Blood-bought: rejoice and be glad in the salvation of thy God.

Rise up ye people of the Lord and show forth His glory: give witness to the redemption of the Lord Jesus.

He hath bought thee with His Blood: by His sacrifice hath he made thee righteous and accepted in the Beloved.

The enemy hath been defeated: glorious stands the assembly of the Blood-bought.

The righteousness of the Lord doth shine forth from His people: in shining white robes shall the Saints of the Lord appear.

Thine iniquity hath been revealed: thou hast turned to the Lord Jesus in faith and He hath raised thee to be partakers of His grace.

Thy sins hath been washed in the Blood of the Lamb and thou hast been made Saints according to His great mercy in redeeming thee.

Lift up thy voices ye Blood-bought Saints and shout forth the greatness of thy God: unto the Lord Jesus give praise and honor to His matchless name.

There is none that can match the mercy of the Lord: His grace is exceeding and abounding.

The Lord is gracious and slow to anger: His mercy is extended to all that call upon His name in faith.

Take up thy garments ye people of the Lord and wash them in the Blood of the Lamb, the Lord Christ: wash thy garments that thou mayest be clothed in the whiteness of His righteousness.

Though thy sins be as scarlet they shall be as wool: though they be red like crimson they shall be white as snow.

Pour forth thy worship ye Blood-bought Saints: give unto the Lord the praises due unto His name.

He hath done marvelous things for thee for He hath redeemed thee and brought thee nigh unto thy God by His Blood.

The world hath rejected the power of the Blood of Jesus: they have eyes but see not the blessing that can be theirs by faith in the atoning work of the Lord.

O the Blood of Jesus, it washes white as snow: nothing can remove sins save the Blood alone.

The world sees not the surpassing power of the Blood: they reject and spurn His redemption.

But the Saints of the Lord rejoice in His Blood: they worship His holiness and praise Him for His sacrifice.

They give glory to their God for the crimson flow of Calvary: to the Lord doth they give their worship for His Blood.

What can wash away my sins: nothing but the Blood of Jesus. What can make me whole again: nothing but the Blood of Jesus.

Rise up ye Blood-bought Saints: rise up and worship His majesty: for the Lord hath redeemed thee and hath called thee by thy name; thou art His.

Psalm 137

Hear the cry of my heart, O God, which doth rise to thee: turn thine ear towards me and hear thou me.

My heart is thy throne room, O Lord, and unto thee alone do I bow.

My soul longs for thee, O God: for a closer more intimate walk with thee doth my soul cry out.

Conform me to the image of the Lord Jesus, O God, I pray: take away all that may distract me or be not according to thy desire for me.

Sanctify thou me, O God: let all that is within me be sanctified by thy power and Presence, O Lord.

My flesh is weak, and I am prone to be sinful: yet by thy power, in thy sanctification, I can stand free from all iniquity and no transgression shall be found in me.

Only by thy power, O Lord, through thy most Holy Spirit may I be sanctified: naught but thy cleansing can set me apart in purity and holiness unto thee, O God.

Hear the longing of my heart of God: hear me that my cry might come upon thine ear.

Thou hast washed me in the Blood and I am clean before thee: yet my soul doth long for a second blessing of thy sanctification.

Purify me, O God, by thy Spirit: place me in the refining fire of thy Spirit and remove all dross from me.

Leave naught but pure gold tried in the fire and ready for thy use, O Lord.

Take away all that doth displease thee that may lodge within me: remove from me all that is not born of thy Spirit and covered in thy Blood.

O Lord, my God, I call upon thy name for thou and thou alone art able to make me what thou wouldst have me be.

I long to do thy will, O God: my soul doth long to walk the pathways of holiness and be sanctified by thee, O God.

I am naught on my own, O God: there doth dwell within me no goodness or purity save by thy Spirit and thy holiness.

Take all of me, O Lord, and conform me to the image of Jesus: let the mark of thy Spirit dwelling within me be seen and let Jesus shine through me.

Thy will, O God, shall forever be my dwelling place: within the glory of thy Presence and thy will shall I ever make my habitation.

Depart from me all ye who art not sanctified: for the Lord is my abode and in Him shall I always find shelter and a holy lodging.

Hear me, O God, that I may be heard: listen to the petition of my heart and turn not thine ear from me.

Break down every barrier in me, O Lord, that doth not conform to thy holiness: tear down any stronghold within me that doth not abide in thy sanctification.

Sanctify me, O God that I may be wholly thine: purify me, O my Lord, that I may be pure: do not turn from me, O God, but hear my cry and empower me by thy Spirit: empower me to thy service, that through thy purity and thy sanctification I may show forth the glory of the Lord Jesus to all the earth.

Thine is the kingdom O God: the power and the glory art thine.

Pour forth the oil of thy anointing upon thy servant, O God. Sanctify me by thy Presence within me through the Holy Ghost.

Let the oil of thy Spirit's Presence flood over me, O Lord, and sanctify thou me: let me be entirely sanctified by thy Presence and power, O Lord, that I may be completely thine.

Psalm 138

Thanks be unto thee, Lord Jesus, for the assurance of full and free salvation by thy grace and mercy.

Before I even asked for help or sought a way out of my sins thou hast already seen me and loved me and gave thy Blood for my redemption.

Though thou didst die more than two thousand years before my birth, yet by thy grace, I know that when thou didst go to the cross to die, that I was on thy mind.

I am blessed beyond measure by the assurance of my Home in heaven and a place by thy Throne, O my God and King.

I long to see thy face, my Lord, I long to see thee: and in seeing thee, bow before thee and say unto thee, "Thanks be to thee Lord Jesus for saving me."

My soul is ever light and joyous for the salvation bought for me by my God and Savior: His Blood hath bought be a Home in Glory with Him.

How could I ever praise thee enough, O my God, for what thou hast done for me?

How can this poor tongue give thee enough worship and praise for thou art worthy of all the praise, all the glory and all the worship that thy servant canst give unto thee.

Heaven is my Home and I long to stand in the Presence of the Holy One and there before the Throne proclaim, saved by grace, saved by love, saved by the Blood: O glory, Hallelujah, I am saved, saved, saved!

No dread of death is on me. No fear of what lies beyond this mortal coil doth chill by soul for the Lord hath extended to me His grace and by His precious Blood am I saved.

Hallelujah to the Lamb: Hallelujah to the Holy One. Glory to the name of Jesus: His name be praised, Hallelujah. Amen.

I am redeemed by love divine. Glory, glory thou art mine.

The King of Heaven hath bought me. I am His and He is mine. Glory, glory, glory to His name.

I will forever lift mine eyes to Calvary: for Calvary paid it all and the empty tomb destroyed the power of death, hell, and the grave.

My soul rejoices in the Lord my God: to the name of Jesus be glory and honor, dominion, and power.

I seek a land both light and fair where darkness hath no part. A land wherein the sainted dwell, the reward of faithful heart.

I look with hope to jasper walls, and seas of crystal hues; I look with faith to pearled gates 'til they come into view.

I've traveled many weary miles; my goal is yet in sight, for in my spirit now I see that City full of Light.

My place therein was purchased by God's own love shed Blood: My mansion there is builded beyond life's tempestuous flood:

'Twill not be long and I shall stand before the Holy Throne, and there proclaim as 'nere before, "Thank God, I now am Home!"

Thanks be unto thee, Lord Jesus, for thy assurance of Heaven and my name in the Book of Life: glory unto thy holy name, O my God.

Psalm 139

Trust in the Lord for He is Truth: the Lord cannot lie neither is there any falsehood in Him.

The Lord is faithful and just: His mercy is extended to all who call upon Him in faith.

Lift up the Lord and make high His name: His name is glorious beyond description.

Put forth thy trust in the Lord of Hosts for His arm is not shortened neither is His power diminished.

The souls of the righteous rejoice in the Lord: they have confidence in His Word and in His power do they place their conviction.

The Lord, the God of heaven and earth hath given His Word and in His verity can all men trust.

Place thy trust in the name of the Lord and in His truth shalt thou be upheld.

Let thy life be guided by the Spirit of the Most Holy One and He shall bring about in thee a new nature: all iniquity shall He place in His forgetfulness and all transgressions shall He no longer remember.

The Spirit of the Lord shall clothe thee in righteousness: in the white robes of His holiness shalt thou be clad.

No man shall achieve his own righteousness but in the Spirit of the Lord all the Blood-bought saints shall be made holy.

Put thy trust in the Lord for He is faithful and true: the Lord is the God of all verity, no dishonesty or deception can be found in Him.

The Lord, the Holy One is ever dependable: He is devoted to His saints and all the Blood-bought shall acknowledge His trustworthiness.

None shall be laid low if they put their confidence in the Lord, the One God of all creation and life.

The Lord is great in power and awesome in His majesty: His love hath been manifested in the Christ and none that call upon His name shall ever be ashamed.

The people of the Lord are exalted by the Spirit of the Lord: in the Holy Ghost shall they ever delight.

The joy of the Lord is the strength of His people and in His Presence, by His Spirit, shall they ever be glad.

They shall dance and shout and unto His name shall they ever give praise: for the Lord is their God, and Jesus is His name.

In the name of the Lord there is great power: the name of the Lord breaks every yoke and destroys the power of the evil one.

Put not thy trust in governments or earthly authorities: for the Lord God is King over all the universe and in His hand is the fate of the whole earth.

Put not thy trust in the power of man for man is as a breath: as a single tick on the clock is the life of a man.

But the Lord is eternal: His power is over all and nothing can diminish His power nor His might.

Trust in the Lord with all thy heart and lean not unto thine own understanding: put thy trust only in Him and He shall make all thy journeying straight.

The Lord shall forever be faithful to His people and in His name shall the righteous ever rejoice and be glad.

Psalm 140

I will shout to the Lord, Hallelujah! Amen.

I will glorify the name of the Lord: Honor and praise Jesus my God.

The Lord shall forever be my song and my rejoicing: in Him am I blessed, and I will shout Hallelujah to the Lord!

The Lord is High and Mighty: glory to His name.

The Lord is Righteous and Holy: Praise to His majesty.

The Lord is Truth and Verity: Hallelujah. Amen.

I will lift up my hands in praise unto thee O Lord: blessed be thy glorious name, O my God.

I will lift up my voice and cry, Holy: the praises of the Lord shall continually flow from my lips.

My feet shall dance to the wonders of His reverence and I shall pay homage to His splendor.

Hallelujah, Jesus! Blessed be thy name.

Hallelujah, Holy One: thou art beyond description: thy majesty is awesome and thy brilliance outshines the sun.

Forever and ever shall I give glory to the Lord for He alone is worthy of all praise and honor: dominion and power are thine, O Lord.

O my God, I long to give thee glory as thou art worthy: yet my lips are weak and my tongue unable to do according to thy holiness.

I will rise up and shout: I will lift up my voice and declare the wonders of the Lord.

Thou art altogether glorious, O my God: Lord Jesus to thee do I give my love and mine adoration.

To thy name, O Lord, do I give praise: unto thee, O Lord, do I give my worship and adoration.

Because of who thou art, O God, do I praise thee: because of who thou art do I give glory.

Only because of thee do I lift up my voice: because of thy wondrous splendor do I shout, Hallelujah!

Thou art my God, my Lord, my Savior, my Jesus, my King: thou art all in all to me, O my God.

I will shout to the Lord, Hallelujah! I will shout to the Lord, glory, glory to thy name.

Throughout eternity I shall sing thy praises: I will worship thee forever, O my God.

Thou art my triumph, O my Lord: thou art the sustenance of my soul and the wonder of my life.

I shall ever praise thee, O God, for all of who thou art: thy glory shall continually be the praise of my heart.

Psalm 141

Testify ye saints: speak forth the wondrous workings of the Lord.

Stand up in the congregation and give glory to the One that hath given thee full and free salvation.

Nothing could take away thy sins save the Blood of the Anointed One: give Him honor for His grace.

Raise up thy hands ye Blood-bought and shout the praises of the Lord thy God.

Testify ye saints: cry forth that thy name hath been written in the Lamb's Book of Life.

Lift up thy voice and shout to the Lord: shout His mercy and His grace: tell forth the love of God, which is shed abroad in our hearts by the Holy Ghost.

In the assembly of the saints will I stand and testify: Jesus saved my soul.

Within the Flock shall I speak forth the compassion of the Shepherd that hath led me from darkness into His marvelous light: who hath brought me from death and hath given unto me eternal life through Christ Jesus my Lord.

Testify ye saints: testify of His forgiveness, His understanding, and His benevolence towards thee for His love's sake.

Rise up in the meeting place and testify of the grace of the Lord: stand up and give forth the praises of the Lord God Almighty, Maker of heaven and earth and Savior of souls.

In the midst of the worshippers give glory unto God: in the center of the parishioners give Him praise.

Worry not of those around thee. Think not of others opinions: concentrate only on the Lord thy Savior and testify of His salvation by His Blood.

The angels cannot sing the song of the redeemed: only those that have been washed in the Blood can sing the song of salvation.

Lift up thy voice ye Blood-bought saints and sing the song of salvation: lift up thy voice and sing of His mercy and grace.

Testify of His goodness and His love: testify of His compassion and His healing: of His touch and His anointing give thou voice unto His glory.

Jesus is worthy: Jesus is worthy: the angels cry out holy, holy, holy but the saints cry out salvation by His Blood, eternal life by His Blood, restoration by His Blood.

Testify ye saints: testify ye Blood-bought: testify ye redeemed for the Lord thy God, Jesus the Christ is worthy of all praise: worthy of all glory and honor: worthy of thy testimony, O ye saints of the Lord.

Forever shall the saints of God lift up the banner of the Lord: forever shall the saints hold up the Blood-stained banner of their God.

Forget thyselves O people of the Lord: forget thyselves and give praise to the Lord thy Savior.

Think not of thy self, thou who hast been washed in the Blood: but give glory unto Jesus: give praise to the One that hath saved thee.

Testify ye saints. Testify of the love of God in Christ Jesus: testify ye saints. Praised be the name of the Lord, Jesus the Anointed One of God, our Savior and Lord: testify ye saints.

Psalm 142

Have mercy on me, O Lord, have mercy.

I am undone and my soul is in despair. Have mercy on me, O Lord.

My sins are ever before mine eyes: I am reminded constantly of my past.

I know thy Blood hath cleansed me. I know my sins are purged. Yet my memories persist and I see all that I have done against thee and thy Word and I am ashamed. Have mercy on me.

Bring forth in me thy power, O my God: let thy Spirit renew in me the conviction of my forgiveness and thy mercy towards me.

The enemy worketh against me: he hath not forgotten that which, in thy glory, thou hast cast into the sea of thy forgetfulness. Have mercy on me, O Lord.

Quicken me, O God, by the Holy Ghost and bring forth in me the joy of thy salvation.

Thou hast cleansed me. Thou hast washed me in the Blood of the Lamb. Thou hast cast my sins as far as the east is from the west, yet my soul is vexed with memories: my heart is brought low with shame and regret.

Take from me, O my God, the shame of my past: erase from my heart those things that thou hast forgotten.

The enemy seeks to lay blame upon me: he doth seek to discourage my soul and draw me away from thee.

Thou and thou alone art my God, and I will forever give thee praise for thy faithfulness and thy grace. Thy mercy doth well within me and I am refreshed by the touch of thy Presence.

Let not the enemy speak guilt into mine ear: allow not his ability to bring back to my remembrance that which is under the Blood: that which thou in thy infinite grace hath washed away and hath made me as if I had never sinned.

O Lord, thou art mine only refuge: thou art the Rock that my trust is placed in: thou art the One in whom I continually place my confidence.

In thee I am reborn and renewed. In thee I am sanctified and pure.

Thy Blood hath made me a new creation in Christ Jesus my Lord: thy Blood hath removed my sins.

I am clothed in the white robes of thy righteousness; O thou my Lord and thy Presence doth renew my spirit.

I cried unto the Lord for mercy and He heard me: I didst call unto my God and He didst answer me.

Thanks be unto God for His infinite mercies and grace: His lovingkindness and tender mercies doth make my soul rejoice.

In thee, O Lord, I am reborn: In thee I am continually renewed.

Thou hast surrounded me with thy Spirit and hath filled me with thy Presence, and I am free from all guilt and shame.

My past is past: my sins are purged: my spirit is renewed by the Holy Ghost and I am washed in the Blood of Jesus.

Naught can touch me with shame: thou hast conquered, O Lord. Thou hast cast out the enemy and in thee, O my God, do I ever rejoice.

I've been washed in the Blood. I am clean. I am whole. I am made new.

I cried unto the Lord and He heard me: from His Holy Hill hath he lifted up His hand and banished the enemy from my presence: the Lord hath had mercy upon me. Blessed be His name forevermore.

Psalm 143

Praise ye the Lord. Praise Him in His sanctuary: praise Him in the heights.

Give praise to the Lord and magnify His name: for the Lord is a great and mighty God full of power and glorious in might.

Praise ye the Lord, O ye saints of the Lord: praise Him in the congregation: praise Him in the meeting place of the righteous.

Exalt the Lord and give honor to His name: bless Him and glorify His holiness.

The earth is the Lord's and all that exists is His: the Lord has the heavens as His throne room and the earth as His footstool.

Praise ye the Lord for His mercy: praise Him for His wondrous grace.

Give thanks unto the Lord and bless His name: for the Lord is merciful to His people and a just and righteous Judge of all.

Give praise unto the name of the Most High for the Lord is a God above all gods: high and holy is He.

Lift up thy voice unto the Lord thy God: give Him the worship of thy heart and glory unto His name.

Praise the Lord for His mercy: praise Him for His love: exalt Him and bless His holy name forever.

Oh that men would praise the Lord for His love towards them: for the Lord is the author of love and in His person He is love Himself.

Praise the Lord ye His saints: give honor and glory unto Him for He is kind and merciful: in His hands are all the names of His saints carved.

The Lord is conscious of all His people: the Lord knoweth all that His saints endure.

The Lord hath turned His ear unto the cry of His people and He doth inhabit their praises.

Cant thou not see? Dost thou not understand? The Lord hath made plain His love: His love brought Him to earth in the likeness of man and for mankind.

By His love He hath bought salvation by the Blood of the Christ.

Give praise unto the Lord for He is worthy: His name is above all names and by His Word doth the universe exist.

Praise ye the Lord: praise Him in the congregation: Praise Him in the Churches: praise Him on the heights: praise Him on the seashore.

Praise the Lord and bless His name: let naught deter thee from exalting the Lord thy God.

Praise Him, O ye people: praise Him, O ye saints. Bless the Lord and make known His greatness throughout the earth.

Praise ye the Lord.

Let the saints of the Lord give forth His praises: worship the Lord in the beauty of holiness.

Dance and rejoice in the sanctuary of the Blood-bought. Lift up thy hands and shout forth the praises of the Lord.

The Lord is great and mighty: high and holy is the Lord God of Hosts.

None there be that can stand higher than the Lord: He is a God of authority and great glory: He is mighty and His name is exalted.

Praise the Lord, ye saints of the Lord: give honor to His name and rejoice in Him forever.

The name of the Lord is glorious in its sounding and mighty in its power.

The name of the Lord giveth salvation to those of faith in Him: His name raises the lame and gives sight to the blind.

The name of the Lord showers power on the infirmed and cureth all their deceases.

Give praise to the Lord for His wondrous power: shout and rejoice for His marvelous healings.

Praise Him ye His people: exalt Him ye His saints: magnify Him all ye Blood-bought ones and celebrate His majesty and power.

Praise ye the Lord.

Psalm 144

When I think about the Lord my soul sings, Glory to His name, glory to His name.

When I think about what the Lord hath done for me, my spirit doth rejoices in His mercy and grace.

The Lord hath taken me from the depths of my sin and hath made me part of His Beloved.

Sin scarred my being and overwhelmed me with mine own transgressions, but the Lord was great in His love for me and wondrous in His forgiveness.

I cried unto the Lord and He heard me and removed my transgressions from me and hath washed me in His Blood.

In the depths of my depravity I cried unto the Lord: Jesus, hear me, forgive my sins and be my Lord and He heard me and hath saved my soul.

Thy Word, O God, doth say that thou didst love the world that thou gavest thine only begotten Son that whosoever believeth in Him shouldst not perish but have everlasting life.

My soul doth exalt in thee, O my God: in thy love do I ever rejoice and am glad.

Thy Word hath assured me that nothing can separate me from the love of God that is in Christ Jesus my Lord and in thy Word am I made secure in thy salvation, O thou Most High.

When I think of what the Lord hath done for me, my soul springs forth in song; raising the Blood-stained Banner of the Cross doth I ever resound His grace.

When I think of what my God hath done for me, my spirit doth break forth in praise.

In the Spirit of the Lord do I ever feel like a colt in clover and as a young buck skipping through the forest shall I rejoice in my God.

By the Spirit of the Lord I can run through a troop and jump over a wall: nothing shall be impossible to me empowered by the Holy Ghost, armed with the name of Jesus.

The Lord hath set me as a sentinel: as a watchman on the wall hath I been appointed.

In myself I am as nothing: but when empowered by the Spirit of my God, nothing can stand against me.

Psalm 145

My being hath been tabernacle by the Spirit of the Lord: he hath anointed me to bring forth the Gospel and tear down the strongholds of the enemies of my God.

The oil of the anointing hath flowed over me: my life and my soul hath been saturated by the holy oil of anointing even as Aaron who had the oil run from his beard to the hems of his garments.

The Gospel of my God shall forever be my service and in the power of the Lord shall I ever break forth the Word of my God.

The Blood shall be my sermon and my song: in the power of the Blood of Jesus shall I ever celebrate and delight.

The Lord is the love of my life, and in Him alone do I glory.

Nothing can stand against the power of the Blood: no principality nor power can stand against its might.

The Lord is my strength and my surety: by the power of Jesus' name and the force of His Spirit shall I ever be empowered.

When I stand under the anointing, demons shall flee from my gaze and tremble at the words of my mouth: for the Lord my God hath indwelled me by His Spirit: quake ye enemies of the Cross and trouble not the saints.

Rise up and flee all ye adversaries of holiness for the power of the Blood is against thee.

Hear me, ye opponents of righteousness; the Blood of Jesus is against thee: thou art defeated by His holiness and against His power thou canst not stand.

I shall ever rejoice in the glory of my God and in the power of the name of Jesus shall I ever stand victorious.

Jesus Christ is Lord: let all the earth give Him praise: let the Blood-bought Saints rise up and bless the Lord for His infinite power and authority over all.

When I think of the Lord my God and all that He hath done for me, my soul shall ever rejoice and be glad.

The Lord is a great God and a great King over all the earth: His name shall forever be praised.

Let thy servant give thee praise, O Lord: let the glory of my God forever be my song.

In thy power and in the strength of thy name thy servant is fortified: in my God am I ever strengthened and upheld.

The Church of the Lord Jesus Christ is a force against evil and against all iniquity doth they stand.

The Saints of the Lord are empowered by His Spirit: they have been washed in the Blood of Jesus and by His might doth they stand as a light upon a hillside and a sentinel on a wall.

Tremble, ye enemies of the Cross: quake in fear ye foes of holiness.

The Saints are clothed in the white robes of His righteousness and His glory doth shine through the holiness of His people.

The Word of the Lord is in their lips and the testimony of His grace is ever upon their hearts.

The people of the Lord are as a flock: they follow their Shepherd and hear only His voice.

Yet the flock is a fierce and mighty multitude: they have been washed in the Blood and empowered by the name of Jesus.

The assembly of the holy rise up against iniquity and give testimony to the deliverance of their God.

They shall ever rejoice in the One who hath given them salvation and hath provided for them eternal life through the name of Jesus.

This servant of the Lord shall ever give Him praise and honor: the glory of the Lord shall throughout eternity be my stronghold.

Praise and honor, glory, dominion, and power shall ever be the song of the righteous: holiness unto the Lord shall ever be their anthem.

Psalm 146

Thou art my Comfort, O God. In thee am I forever blessed.

The world doth surround me with their evils and iniquities: the stress, anxiety, and tensions of this life compass me about continually.

But thou, O God, art always close by me: I have only to call upon thy name and thou dost comfort me.

The mention of thy name doth cast out all weights and traumas of this world and doth give me a taste of thy glory by thy Presence.

Thou didst promise that thou wouldst never leave me nor forsake me and I have never seen the righteous forsaken nor their seed begging for bread.

Thou art ever close by me, O Lord my Lord: thou art n'ere far from me.

My soul is laid low in the pressures of life but the Lord is the uplifter of mine head.

Oft I feel far from thy Presence, O Lord: the world surrounds me with iniquity and unrighteousness is ever before mine eyes.

But my heart is thine, O my God: my life is thine and my heart is thy throne-room.

Nothing that doth come against me shall 'ere deter me from worshipping and serving thee, O thou Most High, my Lord and my God.

I feel the weight of sin surrounding me and the heaviness of mine own inadequacy is ever before mine eyes: yet thou, Lord Jesus, doth bring me comfort and reassurance: thou doth shed thy love abroad in my heart by thy Most Holy Spirit.

Thou doth ease my soul, O Lord: thou dost calm my anxieties and doth soothe my ravaged soul.

Unto thee O Lord shall I ever flee in times of distress: unto the name of my Lord Jesus the Christ shall I ever run for security and relief.

Thou art my God, and I praise thee: thou art my Lord and I shall forever worship thee.

Thou dost give me grace continually and doth compass me about with thy love and mercy.

Unto thee, O Lord, shall I ever run for consolation and solace: thy name Lord Jesus shall ever be my sure and strong tower of strength.

Naught that doth assail me shall draw me from thee, O Lord my God, my Savior, and my King.

Jesus, my Lord, shall forever be my security: in the name of Jesus shall I ever be at ease.

Thou dost n'ere forsake me, O Lord my Lord: thou art ever in tuned unto my call.

When I speak the name of Jesus all of life's anxieties and problems melt into nothingness in the Presence of my God.

Thou, O Lord doth raise me above the troubles of life and by thy Presence and thy Spirit doth thou surround me with thy love.

The Lord shall ever be my refuge and strength and unto the name of my God shall I ever flee in times of trouble.

To Jesus, my God, shall my heart ever turn and unto thy name shall I ever give praise and glory for thou art my God and in thec I am encouraged and my heart is strengthened.

Blessed is the name of the Lord forevermore.

Psalm 147

My heart doth overflow with thanksgiving unto the Lord my God.

Forever shall I give praise unto His name for all that He hath done for me.

The Lord hath given me eternal life through Jesus Christ my Lord and unto His name shall I ever give praise.

Thy grace, O Lord, doth surround me and thy mercy is ever before me.

Though I dwell in a land of iniquity, the Lord shall forever be my assurance and strength.

Unto thee, O Lord shall I ever give my thanks and I shall ever praise thee for thy goodness shown unto me.

The Lord Jesus, my God, shall forever be my worship: His name shall ever be the destination of my praise.

I was low and undone: lost in iniquity and the degradation of my sins and yet Jesus didst love me and give Himself for me.

My life was purchased by the Blood of my Lord and unto His name shall I ever give praise.

Begone from me ye people of iniquity: ye who blaspheme the name of my God get thee gone from my presence.

For the Lord God of Hosts, the Lord Jesus is a God of love and mercy, yet He is ever just and true.

The Lord is a righteous Judge who shall never wink at sin or disregard transgressions.

The Lord is not willing that any should perish nor that any shall find their place in the lake of fire.

But the Lord is a righteous Judge and no iniquitous man shall ever be allowed into His Presence.

The Lord is holy: His robes doth shine as the sun and His eye flash as lightning.

The Lord is holy: His glory is the temple of His people and in His name do they ever rejoice.

Thanks be unto thee, O Lord, for all that thou hast done.

For thy love and thy grace do I praise thee: for the mercy that doth encompass me shall I ever give thee the praises of my heart.

Thou art my God and my King and unto thee shall I ever give thanks.

The rivers of my praise shall ever flow unto thy throne, O Lord.

To thee, O my God, shall I continually lift up my voice and give thee my thanks.

Whilst breath is within me shall I ever proclaim the glories of the Lord my God.

As long as thou dost allow me to live, O Lord, shall I forever give thee praise.

Thou hast bought me with the extreme price of thy Blood, Lord Jesus, and in thee shall I ever rejoice and be glad.

Thy salvation is my strength, O Lord: in the hope of Heaven shall I ever put my trust.

Thou art my God and I praise thee: thou art my Lord and in thee shall I ever delight.

I am a pilgrim in a strange land: as a wanderer in an unknown place am I: for Heaven is my Home and in the Presence of my God shall I ever dwell.

At the foot of the Throne of my Lord Jesus shall I spend eternity giving thee my thanks: unto thy name, O my God shall I worship throughout all eternity.

The first ten thousand years shall I dance before thy Throne, O Lord: and throughout the rest of time without end shall I ever rejoice in the salvation of the Lord Jesus, my Savior, Lord and God.

Psalm 148

Thou hast shown me favor, O God, and my soul doth rejoice in thee.

In the sanctuary of the righteous will I lift up my hands in praise to thy Holy Name.

The raising of my hands doth show my surrender to thy majesty, O Lord and doth give thee the glory that thou art most deserving of.

O Lord, my God, thou art so good to me: they benefits are ever shown forth in my life and I glorify thee.

Hear, O ye people, how the Lord hath shown favor unto His servant.

Harken unto my voice and hear how the blessings of the Lord hath been bestowed upon me.

No good in me doth exist apart from the Presence of He who first loved me and gave himself for me.

The Lord hath disregarded mine iniquity and my transgressions and hath loved me with an overwhelming love.

The love of the Lord hath raised me from the depths of my sins into His glorious light and hath made me accepted in the Beloved by the Blood of Jesus and the empowering of the Holy Spirit.

Come ye iniquitous and kneel at the Cross: come believing that Jesus is the Christ, and that by His death and resurrection thou canst have eternal life.

Let faith arise in thy hearts all ye who come to the Cross and let the Holy Ghost bring saving faith into thy heart that thou mayest be saved.

This unworthy man laid bare his soul before the Holy One and He removed my transgressions from me, washing me in the Blood of Jesus and sanctifying me by the Holy Ghost.

Hear my words, all ye people: harken unto my voice that thou mayest know that God, the Eternal One hath shown His love for thee, by taking on the form of His own creation and giving His life for thee.

The Lord is a God of love; yea, His love hath been shown at Calvary, assured at the empty tomb and shed abroad in our hearts by the Holy Ghost.

The Lord is a God of compassion for none there be that are worthy of His grace and His mercy: yet unto all mankind hath he offered free and full salvation and eternal life through Jesus Christ our Lord.

Thou art truly magnificent, O Lord my God: thou art forever to be praised for who thou art and what thou hast done in the provision of salvation to all who call upon thee in faith.

The working of thy grace is amazing unto thy servant, O Lord my Lord: how thou hast shown thy grace unto me doth ever make my heart rejoice in thee.

Let the saints of the Lord arise and praise His holiness: let the Blood-bought stand up in the sanctuary and testify to the glory of the Lord Most High.

Sing, glory to the Lord ye His people: shout the shouts of Hallelujah to the King of the universe.

For the Lord is great and greatly to be praised: let the majesty of His name be exalted by His people and let the saints of the Lord shout for joy in the sanctuary where His name resides.

Bring to the Lord thy repentant heart and allow His Spirit to wash over thee: bring forth the vessel of thy heart and the Lord shall fill thee with His Presence by His most Holy Spirit.

Thou canst glory in the Lord all ye people of the Lord for the joy of the Lord is thy strength and in His name thou canst forever rejoice and be glad.

In the congregation of the saved shall I ever give praise unto the name of the Lord Jesus my God: Unto the name of the Lord shall I forever rise up in praise.

I will lift up my hands unto thy glory, O Lord, that thou mayest be exalted in my worship of thy holiness.

The Lord hath imparted to me His Spirit and by His Spirit hath His servant been sanctified.

Thanks be unto God for His marvelous working in sanctifying those that come to Him in the white robes of His righteousness and making them partakers in His holiness.

Sing and shout, dance and be glad all ye people of the Name: worship the Lord in the beauty of holiness and exalt His name with thy dancing and rejoicing.

Forsake thy self-consciousness all ye Blood-bought and rise up in worship to the name of the Lord.

Give praise unto God and exalt the name of Jesus for He hath provided for thee full and free salvation by His Blood and complete sanctification by His Spirit.

Forget thyself in praise, O ye people of the Name, and show forth thy joy in singing and in the dance for the Lord is Lord of all and He alone is worthy of all praise.

The Lord God of Host is holy in all His aspects and righteous in all His ways: let the saints celebrate His glory.

Show forth the praises of His name and lift up their voices, their hearts and their hands unto the majesty of His name.

Show forth thy delight in His salvation by thy worship, O ye saints of the Lord: bless His name and make His praise glorious.

Be glad and exult in His salvation, ye people of the Blood and give forth unto the Lord thine adoration and devotion.

Thou, O Lord, hath done marvelously towards thy people: thy love hath bought the faithful and thy Spirit hath provided complete sanctification unto those that come to thee in faith believing.

Thou, O God, art ever ready to bless thy people and to give unto them the glory and power that is in thy name.

Sing praise to the Lord all ye saints: lift up thy voices and bless the Lord.

Show forth thine adoration unto the name of the Lord by thy worship, ye His people and glorify His majesty at all times.

Bring forth the offerings of thy praise, ye saints, and offer unto the Lord the sacrifices of thanksgiving.

Give honor unto His name and show forth thy devotion all ye who love the Lord.

Bring commendations of His holiness before His throne and show forth thy exaltation.

Worship the Lord and give Him praise for He alone is worthy: He alone is worthy of all praise.

Thou, O Lord, hath been gracious unto thy servant and in thee shall I ever rejoice and be glad.

Thou hast shown favor unto me in all my days and with all that is in me shall I bring forth the worship of thy greatness.

Blessed art thou, O Lord my God: holy and righteous art thou forevermore.

Psalm 149

Let praises rise to the heavens: strike up the instruments and break forth in music to glorify the name of the Lord our God.

Sound the trumpets and blast forth on the horns: use stringed instruments and cymbals, wood blocks and tambourines.

Play upon the organ and piano: let the keyboards bring forth sweet music of praise unto the Lord.

Lift up thy voices ye daughters of the Name: lift up thy voices and sing to the glory of the Lord.

Sound forth with thy voices ye sons of God and bless His Name with thy singing.

For the Lord is a great and merciful God and His grace hath been shed upon thee.

Sing and rejoice, sound forth in singing and magnify His name.

The Lord hath done marvelously towards thee, all ye saints of the Lord, and thy voices shouldst be raised unto His majesty and glory.

Rise up and play upon all instruments that the Lord might be praised: let the sweet sounds of music resound throughout the sanctuary of our God.

Rise upon thy feet and dance before His Presence: as the Lord hath blessed thee, so shouldst thou bless the Lord.

Twirl and dance, shout and sing for excellent is His Presence and spectacular is His name.

The Lord is great and remarkable: He is superb in all His doings and amazing in His power.

The people of the Lord shouldst continually praise His sovereignty and His power and shouldst glorify His name in all the earth.

When thou comest together, ye saints of the Lord, thou shouldst be ready to praise His name and worship His majesty.

There is no name like the name of Jesus: no other name hath the power of His name and he is worthy of all praise.

Awe-inspiring is the Presence of the Lord and His people shouldst rejoice in His name.

Let thy praises ring out as bells of a Cathedral that the Lord thy God mayest be glorified and His name exalted.

Sing unto the Lord the song of His redemption: let the redeemed raise up His banner and sing the wonders of His Blood.

Let the instruments sound the praises of His wonderful love and the glories of His mighty name.

Ring out on the cymbals the triumph of our God: let the trumpets sound His awesome majesty and glory.

Shake the tambourines and strike the harps, break forth in singing and dancing to magnify the wonders of the Risen One, Jesus the Christ, the Holy Lord God Almighty.

The angels declare His holiness: the cherubim fly around the Throne crying forth that He is holy: but only the Blood-bought can sing the songs of the redeemed: only those washed in the Blood of Jesus can sing the songs of salvation.

Clothed in the white robes of the righteousness of Christ Jesus: let the saints sing His praises and rejoice in Him.

Let the song of Holiness Unto the Lord ring out continually in the congregations of the righteous for the Lord hath commanded ye be holy as He is holy.

Cry out, ye sanctified ones, and give praise unto the Lord: for the Lord Jesus Christ was crucified yet risen again He lives forever and ever.

Let the music of salvation through the Blood flow from the instruments and hearts of all the saints of God.

Praise His name and be glad in His Presence: bless Him ye people and glorify Him all ye Blood-washed.

Sing forth thy love to the Lord Christ and magnify His mighty name with thy songs of His holiness.

The Lord is glorious beyond description and majestic beyond understanding, yet the people of the Lord shouldst sing forth His praises.

Blessed forever is the name of Jesus: glorious is the name of our God forever and ever, world without end.

Psalm 150

Praise the Lord all ye people: praise and magnify His holy name.

Praise the Lord ye His hosts: glorify His holiness.

Praise the Lord in song: praise Him with instruments and the dance.

Praise Him in the heights: praise Him in the valleys and on the mountain tops.

Praise Him in the sanctuary of the righteous: praise Him in thy secret prayer closets.

Praise the Lord with the trumpet: praise Him with organs and drums.

Praise Him with tambourines and coronets: praise Him with dancing and great jubilation.

Praise the Lord ye His saints: praise Him ye sons and daughters of the Name.

Praise the Lord with the shouts of salvation: praise Him with the cry of the sanctified.

Praise the Lord with instruments: with all instruments of music give praise unto the Lord.

Praise the Lord for His wonders: praise Him for His creation and His handiwork.

Praise the Lord for His mercy: praise Him for His grace.

Praise the Lord for His love: for His lovingkindness give glory unto His Name.

Praise the Lord for His compassion: praise Him for His kindness.

Praise the Lord ye people of faith: praise the Name of Jesus and give glory unto His Name.

Praise Him in the cities: praise Him in the wildernesses.

Praise Him in the congregations: praise Him in meeting places of the saints.

Praise Him in the plains and in the low places give Him glory.

Praise Him on the mountain sides and upon the peaks proclaim His majesty and might.

Praise the Lord for His power: praise Him for the strength of His right arm.

Praise the Lord for all His benefits: for all that He hath done for thee give praise unto His Name.

Praise the Lord and proclaim His holiness: give glory to His righteousness and His justice.

Praise the Lord all His saints and declare the wonders of His Name throughout all the earth.

Praise the Lord in thy private devotions: praise Him with testimonies in the assembly of the Blood-bought.

Praise the Lord in the secret place: praise Him in the open congregations.

Praise the Lord with thy singing and with thy feet, dance before Him to magnify His Name.

Praise the Lord all ye saints: praise Him all ye people of the Blood.

Praise the Lord for His healing: for His stripes hath bought thy healing.

Praise the Lord for His blessings: praise Him for His continuing care.

Praise Him for He is God: praise Him for He alone is the Holy One.

Praise the Lord for who He is for He alone is thy crown and thy salvation.

Praise the Lord all the saved: praise Him for He is God. Blessed be His name forevermore. Amen.